Rewire Your ADHD Brain

A Guide to Better Focus and Productivity

By
Ugochukwu Uche MS., LPC ADHD Coach

Copyright © 2025 by Ugochukwu Uche MS., LPC ADHD Coach

All rights reserved. No part of this publication may be reproduced, stored or transmitted in any form or by any means, electronic, mechanical, photocopying, recording, scanning, or otherwise without written permission from the publisher. It is illegal to copy this book, post it to a website, or distribute it by any other means without permission.

Table of Contents

Introduction: Your Journey to Better Organization and Productivity 1

Part I: Understanding ADHD in Adults 5

1. What is ADHD? 6
2. The Adult ADHD Brain: Focus on the Prefrontal Cortex 21
3. Common Challenges and Misconceptions 36
4. The Power of Lifestyle Changes 52
5. From Awareness to Empowerment 63

Part II: ADHD Success Stories 67

6. Sophia's Story 68
7. A New Beginning with an ADHD Coach 72
8. Empowering Change Through Cognitive Behavioral Strategies 77
9. Sophia's Journey to Mastery 82
10. James' Story 86
11. A New Strategy for Success 91
12. Transforming Challenges into Strengths 96
13. Building Momentum Through Practice 101
14. Laura's Story 106
15. A Blueprint for Balance 110
16. Strategies for a Balanced Life 115

17. Building Resilience Through Practice 120
18. Nathan's Story 125
19. A Roadmap to Balance and Wellness 130
20. Strategies for Sustainable Success 135
21. The Road to Mastery 140
22. Lessons from the ADHD Stories 145

Part III: Nourishing Your Brain 149
23. The ADHD Diet: Whole Foods vs. Processed Foods 150
24. Essential Nutrients for Brain Health 162
25. Meal Planning and Preparation Strategies 173
26. Hydration and Its Impact on Focus 183
27. Supplements and ADHD: What You Need to Know 193
28. Tracking Your Diet and Its Effects 204
29. Worksheets for ADHD Success Strategies 218

Appendix: Additional Resources and Tools for
 ADHD Management 223

References 228

Introduction

Your Journey to Better Organization and Productivity

If you struggle with staying organized, managing your time, focusing on tasks, completing projects, or handling emotional overwhelm and frustration, this book is for you.

As I write this on December 1, 2024, I reflect on recent conversations with four clients who shared frustrations about a shortage of ADHD medications. While I'm not against medication—far from it—it's essential to consider: How long do you plan to rely on it? Weeks? Months? Years? Consider the consequences of disrupted medication access or medication proving less effective than hoped.

Here's the good news: You don't have to depend solely on medication to manage ADHD. You can retrain your brain to work for you instead of against you.

Skeptical? Consider the case of a 29-year-old man who survived a gunshot wound to the brain. This individual was featured in a peer-reviewed study in the American Journal of Case Reports (June 2024).

Imagine surviving a severe brain injury and regaining skills that seemed lost forever. This is exactly what happened to a 29-year-old man who suffered a gunshot wound to the left side of his brain—the area responsible for speech, language, and movement on the right side of the body. Most people would assume such an injury would leave him permanently disabled. But his recovery was nothing short of extraordinary, thanks to the brain's incredible ability to adapt and heal, known as neuroplasticity.

When he arrived at the hospital, he was in a coma and completely unresponsive. Emergency doctors performed life-saving surgery, removing part of his skull to relieve pressure and stop the bleeding in his brain. After the surgery, he was unable to move his right side, speak, or even understand words. His condition seemed hopeless.

But the human brain is not a fixed machine—it can change and rewire itself. Over time, through a structured rehabilitation program, his brain found new ways to work. His right hemisphere began taking over functions once controlled by the injured left side. Slowly, he started to regain movement, communicate, and even recognize words again.

This case is a powerful example of how the brain can adapt and rebuild itself, even after severe damage. Neuroplasticity allows the brain to form new connections and reroute functions when needed. If a person with such a devastating injury can retrain their brain, imagine what you can do with the right ADHD management strategies.

ADHD is also a condition rooted in brain function—it is not a sign of laziness or lack of intelligence. While ADHD can make focus, organization, and productivity more difficult, your brain can change. You can use structured techniques, cognitive strategies, and consistent practice to train your mind to work for you rather than against you.

The science of neuroplasticity shows us that we are not stuck with how our brains work today. With the right approach, you can strengthen your ability to focus, improve time management, and develop better habits. The key is understanding that change is possible and taking small, intentional steps to shape your brain's pathways in ways that support your success.

If a man can rebuild his brain after a life-threatening injury, you can rewire your ADHD brain to reach your full potential. This book will provide a step-by-step process for harnessing the power of neuroplasticity to create lasting change in your life.

Why This Book?

This book is not about quick fixes or wishful thinking. It's about equipping you with science-backed methods grounded in cognitive-behavioral science, neuroscience, and years of real-world experience. As a psychotherapist and ADHD coach with over two decades of experience, I have worked with numerous clients who felt stuck in patterns of distraction and frustration. Repeatedly, I have seen how the right approach can lead to real, lasting change.

What I am offering is a roadmap to better focus and productivity. This step-by-step guide will help you train your brain and create systems that support your success.

Medication vs. Long-Term Skills

Let's be clear: I'm not here to criticize ADHD medication. It can be a powerful tool for managing symptoms but is not a cure. Medication does not teach you how to structure your day, manage distractions, or stay on track with your goals. When the medication wears off or is not accessible, the underlying challenges of ADHD remain.

This book focuses on teaching skills that address these challenges. By harnessing the brain's capacity for neuroplasticity—its ability to adapt and rewire—you can learn to create habits and behaviors that simplify life's demands.

What You Will Achieve

This book will offer you practical, proven techniques to:

- Improving focus by managing distractions and strengthening your attention span.
- Comprehending time management with systems tailored to your needs.

- Building sustainable habits aligned with your goals.
- Reducing emotional overwhelm using mindfulness and stress-reduction strategies.
- Boosting productivity by prioritizing effectively and avoiding procrastination.

Each chapter builds on the last, guiding you through small, manageable steps. You will track your progress, celebrate your wins, and make lasting changes that help you thrive.

The Power of Neuroplasticity

Your brain is not fixed or unchangeable. Like the 29-year-old survivor mentioned earlier, you can harness neuroplasticity to improve your life. Imagine your brain as a network of roads. Right now, some roads may feel like dead ends—disorganization, procrastination, or frustration. But with practice, you can build new pathways leading to focus, productivity, and peace of mind.

Change won't happen overnight. It requires effort, consistency, and patience. However, the rewards—a life where you feel in control, capable, and confident—are worth it.

Let's Begin

You have taken the first step toward change by picking up this book. You are here because you are ready to stop struggling and start thriving. As you read this book, we will work together to help you rewire your ADHD brain and unlock the potential that's always been within you.

Are you ready to begin? Let's get started.

Part I:
Understanding ADHD in Adults

Chapter 1
What is ADHD?

Attention-Deficit/Hyperactivity Disorder (ADHD) is a complex neurodevelopmental disorder that affects millions of people worldwide, both children and adults. Despite its prevalence, many misunderstand, misdiagnose, or overlook ADHD, especially in adults. This chapter aims to provide a comprehensive overview of ADHD, its symptoms, causes, and impact on daily life.

Understanding ADHD

ADHD is characterized by persistent patterns of inattention, hyperactivity, and impulsivity that interfere with daily functioning and development. These symptoms begin in childhood and can continue into adulthood, affecting various aspects of life, including academic performance, work productivity, and personal relationships.

The disorder was officially recognized in the 1960s, but its history dates back much further. In 1798, Scottish physician Sir Alexander Crichton described a condition similar to what we now know as ADHD, noting "mental restlessness" in some of his patients. Throughout the 20th century, the understanding and terminology of ADHD developed from "minimal brain dysfunction" to "hyperkinetic reaction of childhood" before arriving at the current term ADHD in 1987.

The Three Types of ADHD

ADHD is not a one-size-fits-all disorder. It manifests differently in different individuals, and the American Psychiatric Association's Diagnostic and Statistical Manual of Mental Disorders (DSM-5) recognizes three distinct presentations of ADHD:

1. **Predominantly Inattentive Presentation:** Individuals with this type of ADHD struggle primarily with attention-related symptoms. They may appear forgetful, easily distracted, and have difficulty following instructions or completing tasks.

2. **Predominantly Hyperactive-Impulsive Presentation:** This type is characterized by hyperactivity and impulsivity, with fewer attention-related symptoms. Individuals may fidget excessively, have trouble sitting still, and act without thinking.

3. **Combined Presentation:** This is the most common type, where individuals exhibit both inattentive and hyperactive-impulsive symptoms. They struggle with focus and organization while also displaying hyperactive and impulsive behaviors.

It's important to note that these presentations can change over time, and an individual's symptoms may shift as they age. For example, a child who initially presents with predominantly hyperactive-impulsive symptoms may later struggle more with inattention as they enter adolescence or adulthood.

ADHD Symptoms

The symptoms of ADHD fall into two major categories: inattention and hyperactivity-impulsivity. Let's explore each.

Symptoms of Inattention

Inattention in ADHD goes beyond being distracted. It involves difficulty focusing, organizing tasks, and managing time effectively. Some common symptoms include:

- Difficulty paying close attention to details or making careless mistakes in schoolwork, work, or other activities
- Trouble holding attention on tasks or play activities

- Appearing not to listen when spoken to directly
- Failing to follow through on instructions and failing to finish schoolwork, chores, or duties in the workplace
- Difficulty organizing tasks and activities
- Avoiding, disliking, or being reluctant to do tasks that require sustained mental effort
- Losing things necessary for tasks and activities (e.g., school materials, pencils, books, tools, wallets, keys, paperwork, eyeglasses, mobile telephones)
- Being easily distracted
- Being forgetful in daily activities

These symptoms can manifest in various ways. For example, a student with ADHD might forget to turn in homework assignments, even if they have completed them. An adult with ADHD might struggle to manage their time effectively, often running late for appointments or missing deadlines at work.

Symptoms of Hyperactivity and Impulsivity

Hyperactivity and impulsivity in ADHD manifest as excessive movement, restlessness, and hasty actions that occur without thought. Common symptoms include:

- Fidgeting with or tapping hands or feet or squirming in the seat
- Leaving seat in situations when remaining seated is expected
- Running about or climbing in situations where it is not appropriate (in adolescents or adults, this may be limited to feeling restless)
- Unable to play or take part in leisure activities quietly

- Being "on the go," acting as if "driven by a motor"
- Talking excessively
- Blurting out an answer before a question has been completed
- Having trouble waiting for one's turn
- Interrupting or intruding on others

These symptoms might manifest in children as constant motion, difficulty sitting still during meals or school lessons, or a tendency to climb on furniture. In adults, hyperactivity often becomes more internalized, presenting as inner restlessness, fidgeting, or a constant need for activity.

Understanding that everyone may experience some of these symptoms occasionally is crucial. To be diagnosed with ADHD, these symptoms must be persistent, present for at least six months, and inappropriate for the person's developmental level. Additionally, the symptoms must cause significant impairment in social, academic, or occupational functioning.

The ADHD Brain

To truly understand ADHD, it's essential to look at how the ADHD brain differs from a neurotypical brain. Research has identified several key differences in brain structure and function in individuals with ADHD.

Structural Differences

Studies have shown that certain brain regions in people with ADHD may be smaller or develop at a slower rate. These areas include:

- The prefrontal cortex, which is responsible for executive functions like planning, decision-making, and impulse control.
- The basal ganglia, which play a role in controlling voluntary movement and regulating communication within the brain.

- The cerebellum, which is involved in motor control and cognitive functions.

- The corpus callosum, which facilitates communication between the left and right hemispheres of the brain.

Research has found that these structural differences tend to normalize as children with ADHD reach adulthood, suggesting that ADHD is a delay in brain maturation rather than a permanent difference in brain structure.

Neurotransmitter Imbalances

ADHD is also associated with imbalances in certain neurotransmitters, particularly dopamine and norepinephrine. These chemical messengers play crucial roles in regulating attention, motivation, and impulse control.

Dopamine: People with ADHD typically have lower levels of dopamine in brain regions, including the prefrontal cortex. Dopamine is involved in motivation, reward, and pleasure. Lower levels can lead to difficulty sustaining cognitive functions like attention and impulse control. This dopamine deficiency may explain why individuals with ADHD often seek out stimulating or risky activities, as these can temporarily boost dopamine levels.

Norepinephrine: This neurotransmitter sustains attention and helps with executive functioning. Lower levels of norepinephrine contribute to the attention difficulties seen in ADHD. Norepinephrine also regulates arousal and sleep patterns, which may explain why many individuals with ADHD have sleep problems.

Understanding these neurotransmitter imbalances has been crucial in developing effective treatments for ADHD. Many medications used to treat ADHD work by increasing the availability of dopamine and norepinephrine in the brain.

Executive Function Deficits

One of the hallmarks of ADHD is impairment in executive functions. These are a set of cognitive processes that include:

- Planning and prioritizing
- Impulse control
- Emotional regulation
- Working memory
- Time management
- Cognitive flexibility
- Goal-directed persistence
- Metacognition (self-awareness and self-monitoring)

Individuals with ADHD often struggle with these functions, which can significantly impact their daily lives and ability to achieve long-term goals. For example:

- Difficulty with planning and prioritizing can lead to procrastination and missed deadlines.
- Poor impulse control can result in hasty decisions or inappropriate social behavior.
- Challenges with emotional regulation may cause mood swings or overreactions to minor frustrations.
- Weak working memory can make it hard to follow multi-step instructions or keep track of ongoing tasks.
- Time management issues often lead to chronic lateness and underestimation of the duration of tasks.
- Lack of cognitive flexibility can make it difficult to adapt to changes in routines or expectations.

It's important to note that while individuals with ADHD struggle with these executive functions, they can improve with targeted interventions and strategies.

ADHD Across the Lifespan

While ADHD is often associated with childhood, it's important to recognize that it can persist into adolescence and adulthood. ADHD's manifestation can change over time.

ADHD in Children

In children, ADHD often presents with more visible symptoms of hyperactivity and impulsivity. Common signs include:

- Difficulty sitting still in class
- Interrupting others
- Acting without thinking
- Struggling to follow instructions or complete tasks
- Losing or forgetting school materials
- Daydreaming or seeming "spaced out"

As academic and social demands increase, symptoms of inattention may become more prominent and begin to interfere with school performance and peer relationships. Children with ADHD may struggle to make and keep friends due to impulsive behavior or difficulty following social cues.

It's worth noting that ADHD symptoms in children can sometimes be mistaken for other conditions, such as learning disabilities, anxiety, or oppositional defiant disorder. This underscores the importance of a comprehensive evaluation by a qualified professional.

ADHD in Adolescents

As children with ADHD enter adolescence, hyperactivity symptoms may decrease, but inattention and impulsivity often persist. Teens with ADHD may struggle with:

- Organization and time management
- Completing homework and long-term projects
- Regulating emotions
- Resisting peer pressure
- Maintaining focus during lectures or while studying
- Managing increased academic and social expectations

They may also be more likely to engage in risky behaviors, such as substance use, unsafe sexual activity, or reckless driving. This is partly due to the combination of ADHD-related impulsivity and the natural tendency for risk-taking in adolescence.

Adolescence is also a time when comorbid conditions, such as anxiety or depression, may become more apparent. The increased demands and stresses of teenage life can exacerbate ADHD symptoms and lead to secondary mental health issues.

ADHD in Adults

Many adults with ADHD were not diagnosed in childhood, leading to years of unexplained struggles. In adulthood, ADHD symptoms can manifest as:

- Difficulty with time management and organization
- Procrastination and trouble completing tasks
- Impulsive decision-making
- Mood swings and emotional dysregulation

- Relationship difficulties
- Career challenges
- Financial management issues
- Struggles with self-esteem and self-perception

It's worth noting that adults with ADHD often develop coping mechanisms over time, which can sometimes mask their symptoms. This can make the diagnosis in adulthood more challenging, as the outward signs of ADHD may be less noticeable.

Adult ADHD can significantly impact various life domains. In the workplace, adults with ADHD may struggle with meeting deadlines, staying organized, or maintaining focus during long meetings. In personal relationships, they might face challenges due to forgetfulness, emotional reactivity, or difficulty with long-term planning.

Despite these challenges, many adults with ADHD also report positive aspects of the condition, such as creativity, enthusiasm, and the ability to hyperfocus on topics of interest. With proper support and management strategies, adults with ADHD can lead successful, fulfilling lives.

The Impact of ADHD on Daily Life

ADHD can significantly affect various aspects of an individual's life:

Academic and Professional Impact

People with ADHD often struggle in academic and professional settings due to difficulties with:

- Staying focused during lectures or meetings
- Completing assignments or projects on time
- Organizing tasks and managing time effectively

- Following complex instructions
- Maintaining consistent performance

These challenges can lead to underachievement in school or work despite having the intellectual capacity to succeed. Students with ADHD may receive lower grades or face disciplinary actions frequently due to incomplete work or disruptive behavior. In the workplace, adults with ADHD might struggle with productivity, miss deadlines, or have difficulty advancing their careers.

However, it's important to note that with proper support and accommodations, individuals with ADHD can excel academically and professionally. Many successful entrepreneurs, artists, and innovators have ADHD and attribute some of their success to the unique way their minds work.

Social and Relationship Challenges

ADHD can also affect social interactions and relationships. Individuals with ADHD may:

- Interrupt conversations or have difficulty waiting their turn to speak
- Miss social cues or important details in conversations
- Struggle with emotional regulation, leading to conflicts
- Have difficulty maintaining long-term relationships due to forgetfulness or impulsivity
- Struggle with reciprocity in friendships or romantic relationships

These social challenges can lead to feelings of rejection or isolation. Children with ADHD may have trouble making and keeping friends, while adults might struggle with romantic relationships or professional networking.

However, many people with ADHD also possess positive social traits, such as enthusiasm, creativity, and a good sense of humor, which can enhance their relationships when properly channeled.

Mental Health Comorbidities

People with ADHD are at higher risk for other mental health conditions, including:

- Anxiety disorders
- Depression
- Substance use disorders
- Learning disabilities
- Oppositional Defiant Disorder (in children)
- Conduct Disorder (in adolescents)
- Bipolar Disorder
- Personality Disorders (in adults)

These comorbidities can complicate diagnosis and treatment, making it crucial for individuals with ADHD to receive comprehensive mental health care. The presence of these co-occurring conditions can exacerbate ADHD symptoms and vice versa, creating a complex interplay of mental health challenges.

It's estimated that up to 80% of adults with ADHD have at least one coexisting psychiatric disorder over their lifetime. This high rate of comorbidity underscores the importance of thorough assessment and individualized treatment plans.

Diagnosing ADHD

Diagnosing ADHD is a complex process that requires a comprehensive evaluation by a qualified healthcare professional. There is no single test that can definitively diagnose ADHD. Instead, diagnosis typically involves:

1. **Medical History:** A thorough medical, family, and personal history review. This includes exploring the onset and duration of symptoms, as well as any family history of ADHD or related conditions.

2. **Symptom Assessment:** Using standardized rating scales and checklists to evaluate ADHD symptoms. These might include the ADHD Rating Scale, the Conners' Rating Scales, or the Brown Attention-Deficit Disorder Scales.

3. **Physical Exam:** This is to rule out other medical conditions that might explain the symptoms. It might include tests for vision and hearing problems, sleep disorders, or thyroid issues.

4. **Psychological Evaluation:** This is used to assess cognitive abilities and screen for other mental health conditions. It might involve intelligence tests, personality assessments, or screenings for anxiety and depression.

5. **Information from Multiple Sources:** For children, this often includes reports from parents and teachers. For adults, it may be input from partners or family members. This helps establish that symptoms are present in multiple settings, a key diagnostic criterion for ADHD.

6. **Developmental Assessment:** To ensure that the individual's behavior is inappropriate for their developmental stage.

7. **Consideration of Alternative Explanations:** The healthcare provider will consider whether another condition, such as anxiety, depression, or a learning disability, might better explain the symptoms.

It's important to note that the criteria for diagnosing ADHD differ slightly between children and adults:

- Children up to 16 years must show at least six symptoms of inattention, hyperactivity, impulsiveness, or both.
- Adults and youth over 16 years must show at least five symptoms of inattention, hyperactivity, impulsiveness, or both.

These symptoms must be present for at least six months, occur in multiple settings (e.g., home and school/work), and significantly impair daily functioning.

The diagnostic process for ADHD in adults can be particularly challenging, as it requires retrospective assessment of childhood symptoms. Many adults seeking diagnosis may not have clear memories of their childhood behaviors, and childhood records or observer reports may not be available.

It's also worth noting that ADHD often looks different in girls and women compared to boys and men. Girls are more likely to have inattentive-type ADHD, which may be less noticeable than the hyperactive-impulsive type more common in boys. This can lead to underdiagnosis or misdiagnosis in females.

ADHD is a complex neurodevelopmental disorder that affects individuals across their lifespan. It's characterized by persistent inattention, hyperactivity, and impulsive patterns that can significantly impact various aspects of life. Understanding ADHD involves recognizing its diverse presentations, the underlying brain differences, and how symptoms can change over time.

While ADHD presents challenges, it's important to remember that with proper diagnosis and treatment, individuals with ADHD can lead successful, fulfilling lives. Many people with ADHD possess unique strengths, such as creativity, enthusiasm, and the ability to hyperfocus on topics of interest. These qualities can lead to significant achievements in various fields when properly channeled.

Understanding ADHD is the first step towards effective management. It's crucial to recognize that ADHD is not a character flaw or a lack of willpower but a neurobiological condition that affects brain function. With this understanding, individuals with ADHD and their support systems can work together to develop strategies that capitalize on strengths while addressing areas of difficulty.

ADHD treatment typically involves a multimodal approach, combining medication (when appropriate), behavioral interventions, and lifestyle modifications. As we will explore in subsequent chapters, diet, exercise, and cognitive-behavioral strategies can all prove essential in managing ADHD symptoms.

It's also worth noting that societal understanding and acceptance of ADHD have improved over the years, leading to better accommodations in educational and workplace settings. However, there's still work to be done in reducing stigma and increasing support for individuals with ADHD.

As we progress in this workbook, we will explore practical strategies for managing ADHD symptoms, improving organization, and boosting productivity. Remember, ADHD is a complex condition, and what works best can vary from person to person. The journey to better management is often one of experimentation and personalization.

By understanding what ADHD is, how it affects the brain and behavior, and the various ways it can impact daily life, you have taken the first crucial step toward effectively managing this condition. With knowledge, support, and the right strategies, you can harness your unique potential and thrive with ADHD.

In the following chapters, we will explore specific interventions, starting with dietary changes that support brain health and potentially alleviate ADHD symptoms. We will then move on to behavioral techniques and cognitive strategies to help you build the skills needed for better organization and productivity.

Remember, managing ADHD is a journey, not a destination. Be patient with yourself, celebrate your progress, and don't hesitate to seek support when needed. With persistence and the right tools, you can develop effective strategies to navigate the challenges of ADHD and unlock your full potential.

Chapter 2

The Adult ADHD Brain: Focus on the Prefrontal Cortex

Attention-Deficit/Hyperactivity Disorder (ADHD) is a complex neurodevelopmental disorder that persists into adulthood for many individuals. While ADHD affects various brain regions, the prefrontal cortex (PFC) plays a particularly crucial role in the symptoms and challenges associated with adult ADHD. This chapter will delve deep into the structure, function, and connectivity of the prefrontal cortex in adults with ADHD, exploring how differences in this brain region contribute to the disorder's manifestation.

The Prefrontal Cortex: An Overview

The prefrontal cortex is often described as the "executive center" of the brain. Located at the front of the frontal lobes, it is responsible for a wide range of higher-order cognitive functions, collectively known as executive functions. These include:

1. Attention and focus
2. Planning and organization
3. Decision-making
4. Impulse control
5. Emotional regulation
6. Working memory
7. Time management
8. Cognitive flexibility

In individuals with ADHD, the prefrontal cortex often shows structural and functional differences compared to those without the disorder. These differences contribute significantly to the core symptoms of ADHD: inattention, hyperactivity, and impulsivity.

Anatomical Subdivisions of the Prefrontal Cortex

To better understand the role of the prefrontal cortex in ADHD, it's important to recognize its main subdivisions:

1. Dorsolateral Prefrontal Cortex (DLPFC): This region is crucial for working memory, attention, and cognitive flexibility.

2. Ventrolateral Prefrontal Cortex (VLPFC): Involved in inhibitory control and task-switching.

3. Medial Prefrontal Cortex (mPFC): Important for self-referential processing and social cognition.

4. Orbitofrontal Cortex (OFC): Plays a role in decision-making, especially concerning reward and punishment.

5. Anterior Cingulate Cortex (ACC): While not strictly part of the prefrontal cortex, it's closely connected and involved in error detection and conflict monitoring.

Each of these regions contributes uniquely to executive functioning, and alterations in their structure or function can lead to specific ADHD symptoms.

Structural Differences in the ADHD Prefrontal Cortex

Neuroimaging studies have revealed several structural differences in the prefrontal cortex of adults with ADHD:

1. Reduced Gray Matter Volume

Multiple studies have shown that adults with ADHD tend to have reduced gray matter volume in various regions of the prefrontal cortex. This reduction is particularly notable in:

- Dorsolateral Prefrontal Cortex (DLPFC) – This part of the brain helps with focus, planning, and problem-solving. It's like your brain's manager, helping you stay on track, make decisions, and think through complex tasks.

- Ventrolateral Prefrontal Cortex (VLPFC) – This area helps you control impulses and switch between tasks. It acts like a brake, stopping you from saying or doing something too quickly, and helps you shift your attention when needed.

- Orbitofrontal Cortex (OFC) – This region helps with decision-making and emotional control. It helps you weigh the pros and cons of a choice and regulates emotions so you don't overreact in stressful situations.

These reductions in gray matter volume may contribute to difficulties in executive functioning, as these areas are crucial for attention, impulse control, and decision-making. For instance, a meta-analysis by Frodl and Skokauskas (2012) found consistent reductions in gray matter volume in the right globus pallidus and putamen, regions closely connected to the prefrontal cortex and involved in motor control and learning.

2. Cortical Thickness

Research shows that the outer layer of the brain (cortex) develops differently in adults with ADHD. A study by Shaw et al. (2006) found that people with ADHD experience delayed brain development, especially in the prefrontal cortex, which helps with focus, planning, and self-control. This delay can continue into adulthood, making it harder for the brain's networks to work efficiently.

Interestingly, all brain areas do not develop at the same pace. Some parts, like the motor cortex (which controls movement), may develop faster than normal, while the prefrontal cortex develops more slowly. This uneven brain growth may help explain the mixed symptoms of ADHD, such as difficulty focusing but also high energy levels.

3. White Matter Integrity

The brain's white matter helps different areas of the brain communicate with each other, but research shows that this connection is weaker in adults with ADHD. Diffusion tensor imaging (DTI) studies have found that the pathways linking the prefrontal cortex to deeper brain areas (which control motivation and rewards) do not work as efficiently as they should.

A study by Konrad et al. (2010) found that adults with ADHD had weaker white matter connections in important brain pathways, including the cingulum bundle and superior longitudinal fasciculus. These pathways help the prefrontal cortex connect with other brain areas responsible for attention and decision-making, which may explain why people with ADHD struggle with focus and self-control.

4. Volumetric Differences in Subcortical Structures

Even though they are not part of the prefrontal cortex, some deeper brain areas that work closely with it are also different in people with ADHD. A large study by Hoogman et al. (2017) found that people with ADHD had smaller brain structures in certain areas, including the amygdala (which helps process emotions), the hippocampus (which helps with memory), and the nucleus accumbens (which is involved in motivation and rewards). These size differences may help explain why people with ADHD often struggle with emotions, memory, and motivation.

Functional Differences in the ADHD Prefrontal Cortex

Beyond structural differences, the prefrontal cortex in adults with ADHD also shows altered patterns of activation and connectivity:

1. Hypoactivation During Cognitive Tasks

Functional neuroimaging studies have consistently shown reduced activation in prefrontal regions when adults with ADHD perform tasks requiring executive functions. This hypoactivation is particularly evident in:

- The dorsolateral prefrontal cortex during working memory tasks
- The ventrolateral prefrontal cortex during inhibition tasks
- The anterior cingulate cortex during attention and conflict resolution tasks

This reduced activation may explain the difficulties that adults with ADHD experience in sustaining attention, inhibiting impulses, and managing complex cognitive tasks. For example, a meta-analysis by Cortese et al. (2012) found consistent hypoactivation in fronto-parietal networks during executive function tasks in individuals with ADHD.

2. Altered Functional Connectivity

The prefrontal cortex does not operate in isolation; it's part of more extensive brain networks. In adults with ADHD, there are often alterations in how the prefrontal cortex communicates with other brain regions:

- Reduced connectivity between the prefrontal cortex and the striatum, affecting motivation and reward processing
- Altered connectivity with the default mode network (DMN), which may contribute to difficulties in switching between task-focused and resting states

- Abnormal connectivity with limbic regions, potentially impacting emotional regulation

These brain connection problems can make it harder for people with ADHD to put together information and think clearly. A study by Castellanos et al. (2008) found that adults with ADHD had weaker connections between the part of the brain that focuses on tasks (including the prefrontal cortex) and the part that becomes active when daydreaming or resting (the default mode network). This may explain why people with ADHD often have trouble blocking out their thoughts and staying focused on what's happening around them.

3. Task-Positive and Task-Negative Network Dynamics

The interplay between task-positive networks (which activate during goal-directed tasks) and task-negative networks (which activate during rest) is crucial for cognitive function. In ADHD, the balance between these networks is often disrupted.

In 2007, researchers Sonuga-Barke and Castellanos suggested a theory called the default mode interference hypothesis. They found that people with ADHD may struggle to stay focused because their brain's default mode network—the part of the brain that activates when resting or daydreaming—sometimes turns on during tasks that require attention. This can cause sudden lapses in focus. Their research also showed that the prefrontal cortex plays a key role in managing this process, working with other brain networks to help control attention.

Neurotransmitter Imbalances in the Prefrontal Cortex

The function of the prefrontal cortex is heavily dependent on neurotransmitter systems, particularly dopamine and norepinephrine. In ADHD, there are imbalances in these neurotransmitter systems:

1. Dopamine

Dopamine plays a crucial role in attention, motivation, and reward processing. In adults with ADHD, there is often a deficiency in dopamine signaling in the prefrontal cortex. This can lead to:

- Difficulty sustaining attention on non-rewarding tasks
- Impulsivity and risk-taking behaviors
- Problems with motivation and task initiation

In 2009, researchers led by Dr. Nora Volkow used brain scans to study dopamine activity in adults with ADHD. They found that these individuals had fewer dopamine receptors and released less dopamine in certain brain areas, including the prefrontal cortex. Dopamine is a chemical that helps control attention and motivation. This shortage might explain why people with ADHD often look for exciting or new experiences—to naturally boost their dopamine levels.

2. Norepinephrine

Norepinephrine is involved in arousal, attention, and cognitive processing. Like dopamine, norepinephrine levels are often dysregulated in the ADHD brain. This can result in:

- Difficulties in maintaining alertness and focus
- Problems with working memory and information processing
- Challenges in regulating emotional responses

The interplay between these neurotransmitter systems in the prefrontal cortex is complex, and their dysregulation contributes significantly to the cognitive and behavioral symptoms of ADHD.

3. Other Neurotransmitters

While dopamine and norepinephrine are the primary focus of ADHD research, other neurotransmitters also play a role:

- **Serotonin:** Involved in mood regulation and impulse control
- **Glutamate and GABA:** The balance between these excitatory and inhibitory neurotransmitters is crucial for optimal prefrontal cortex function

Recent research is exploring how imbalances in these neurotransmitter systems might contribute to ADHD symptoms and comorbidities.

The Prefrontal Cortex and ADHD Symptoms

Understanding how the prefrontal cortex's structure and function relate to ADHD symptoms can provide insight into the challenges faced by adults with the disorder:

1. Inattention

The prefrontal cortex, particularly the dorsolateral regions, is crucial for sustaining attention. The reduced activation and altered connectivity in this area can explain why adults with ADHD struggle to:

- Focus on tasks, especially those that are not inherently interesting
- Filter out distractions from the environment
- Switch attention between tasks efficiently
- Maintain organization and follow through on plans

In 2009, researchers led by Fassbender used brain scans to study adults with ADHD during tasks that required them to stay focused. They discovered that these individuals had less activity in the dorsolateral prefrontal cortex—an important part of the brain for maintaining attention. This reduced activity was linked to a higher tendency to get distracted.

2. Hyperactivity and Impulsivity

The ventral and medial portions of the prefrontal cortex are involved in impulse control and behavioral inhibition. Alterations in these regions can lead to:

- Difficulty sitting still or remaining in one place for extended periods
- Talking excessively or interrupting others
- Acting without considering consequences
- Engaging in risky behaviors

In 2010, researchers led by Ana Cubillo used brain scans to study teenagers and adults with ADHD while they performed tasks that required self-control. They discovered that these individuals had less activity in the ventrolateral prefrontal cortex—a part of the brain important for controlling impulses. This reduced activity may help explain why people with ADHD often act impulsively.

3. Executive Function Deficits

The prefrontal cortex is the seat of executive functions, and its altered function in ADHD can result in a range of challenges:

- Poor time management and difficulty estimating time
- Struggles with planning and prioritizing tasks
- Difficulties with working memory, affecting the ability to hold and manipulate information
- Problems with emotional regulation, leading to mood swings or overreactions

In 2005, researchers led by Erik Willcutt analyzed many studies to understand how ADHD affects thinking skills. They found that people with ADHD often have trouble with key mental abilities, including:

- Stopping impulsive actions (response inhibition)
- Staying alert and attentive (vigilance)
- Remembering information temporarily (working memory)
- Organizing and planning tasks (planning)

These difficulties can make it challenging for individuals with ADHD to manage daily activities that require focus and self-control.

The Prefrontal Cortex and ADHD Comorbidities

The prefrontal cortex's role extends beyond core ADHD symptoms. Its altered function can also contribute to common comorbidities seen in adults with ADHD:

1. Anxiety and Depression

The prefrontal cortex plays a role in emotional regulation and mood. Alterations in its function and connectivity with limbic regions can increase vulnerability to anxiety and depression, which are common comorbidities in adult ADHD.

In 2011, researchers led by Dr. Jonathan Posner studied teenagers with ADHD to see how different parts of their brains communicate, especially when processing emotions. They discovered that the connection between the amygdala (the area that handles emotions) and the prefrontal cortex (the area responsible for thinking and decision-making) was different in these individuals. This difference was linked to unusual responses to emotional situations, which might help explain why people with ADHD often experience higher levels of anxiety and depression.

2. Substance Use Disorders

The prefrontal cortex's involvement in impulse control and reward processing makes it relevant to substance use disorders. Adults with ADHD may be more prone to substance abuse due to altered reward sensitivity and difficulties with impulse control.

In 2011, researchers led by Dr. Timothy Wilens studied adults with ADHD and found they were more likely to have problems with alcohol or drugs compared to adults without ADHD. They also discovered that difficulties with executive function—skills like remembering instructions, controlling emotions, and planning tasks—partly explained why individuals with ADHD are more prone to substance use issues.

3. Sleep Disorders

The prefrontal cortex regulates sleep-wake cycles. Alterations in its function can contribute to the sleep disturbances often seen in adults with ADHD.

In 2013, researchers led by Dr. Judith Owens studied sleep in adults with ADHD. They found that these individuals had more sleep problems compared to those without ADHD. These sleep issues were linked to greater difficulties in daily activities.

Neuroplasticity and the ADHD Brain

Despite the challenges associated with prefrontal cortex differences in ADHD, it's important to note that the brain remains plastic throughout life. This neuroplasticity offers hope for improving prefrontal cortex function in adults with ADHD:

1. Medication Effects

Stimulant medications, commonly used to treat ADHD, work by increasing dopamine and norepinephrine availability in the prefrontal cortex. This can improve this region's activation and connectivity, alleviating ADHD symptoms.

In 2013, researchers led by Dr. Timothy Spencer studied how the medication methylphenidate (commonly known as Ritalin) affects adults with ADHD. They found that when these individuals took the medication, there was increased activity in the prefrontal cortex—a part of the brain important for tasks like focusing and organizing. This boost in brain activity was linked to better performance on memory tasks.

2. Cognitive Training

Targeted cognitive training exercises can potentially strengthen prefrontal cortex function. Working memory training, for example, has shown promise in improving executive functions in some adults with ADHD.

In 2005, researchers led by Dr. Torkel Klingberg studied children with ADHD to see if special computer-based exercises could help improve their working memory—the ability to hold and use information in mind. They found that after intensive training, the children's working memory improved, and their ADHD symptoms decreased. Other studies have seen similar benefits in adults, but more research is needed to confirm these findings.

3. Mindfulness and Meditation

Practices like mindfulness meditation have been shown to enhance prefrontal cortex activation and improve attention regulation. These techniques can be valuable adjuncts to traditional ADHD treatments.

In 2008, Dr. Lidia Zylowska and her team studied how an 8-week mindfulness meditation program could help adults and teenagers with ADHD. After the program, participants noticed better attention control and found it easier to manage their thoughts. They also reported feeling less anxious and depressed.

4. Lifestyle Factors

Regular exercise, adequate sleep, and stress management can all positively impact prefrontal cortex function. These lifestyle factors can support overall brain health and potentially mitigate some ADHD symptoms.

In 2015, Dr. Betsy Hoza and her team studied young children at risk for ADHD to see if regular physical activity could help. They found that children who engaged in regular aerobic exercise showed better thinking skills and had fewer ADHD symptoms. Although it's believed that regular physical activity may also benefit adults, more studies are needed to confirm this.

Future Directions in ADHD Brain Research

As our understanding of the prefrontal cortex in ADHD continues to evolve, several exciting areas of research are emerging:

1. Personalized Medicine

Advances in neuroimaging and genetic research may soon allow for more personalized treatment approaches. By identifying specific patterns of prefrontal cortex dysfunction, clinicians may be able to tailor interventions more effectively to individual patients.

2. Novel Treatment Approaches

New treatments targeting prefrontal cortex function are being explored. These include non-invasive brain stimulation techniques like transcranial magnetic stimulation (TMS) and transcranial direct current stimulation (tDCS).

3. Developmental Trajectories

Longitudinal studies are providing insights into how ADHD-related brain differences change over the lifespan. This research may help identify critical periods for intervention and improve our understanding of why some individuals "outgrow" ADHD symptoms while others do not.

4. Integration of Multiple Neurobiological Models

While this chapter has focused on the prefrontal cortex, it's essential to recognize that ADHD involves multiple brain networks. Future research will likely focus on integrating our understanding of prefrontal cortex dysfunction with other neurobiological models of ADHD, such as the default mode network interference hypothesis and theories of altered reward processing.

The prefrontal cortex plays a central role in the neurobiology of adult ADHD. Its structural and functional differences contribute significantly to the disorder's core symptoms and associated executive function deficits. Understanding these differences provides valuable insights into why adults with ADHD struggle with attention, impulse control, and organization.

However, it's crucial to remember that ADHD is a complex disorder involving multiple brain regions and networks. While the prefrontal cortex is a key player, it's just part of a larger neurobiological picture. The interactions between the prefrontal cortex and other brain areas, such as the striatum, limbic system, and default mode network, are equally important in understanding the full spectrum of ADHD symptoms.

This understanding of the prefrontal cortex can be empowering for adults living with ADHD. It highlights that their struggles are rooted in brain differences, not character flaws or lack of willpower. Moreover, the brain's plasticity offers hope for improvement through various interventions and lifestyle changes. From medication and cognitive training to mindfulness practices and physical exercise, there are multiple avenues for potentially enhancing prefrontal cortex function and mitigating ADHD symptoms.

As research in this field advances, we can expect more refined and targeted interventions. Depending on individual patterns of brain function and connectivity, personalized medicine approaches may allow for more effective treatment strategies. Novel technologies, such as neurofeedback and non-invasive brain stimulation, offer promising avenues for directly modulating prefrontal cortex activity.

It's also important to recognize that while the prefrontal cortex differences in ADHD present challenges, they may also confer specific strengths. Some adults with ADHD report enhanced creativity, an ability to think outside the box, and a talent for hyper-focusing on tasks they find engaging. Understanding the neurobiology of ADHD should not only focus on addressing deficits but also on harnessing these potential strengths.

The study of the prefrontal cortex in adult ADHD provides a window into the complex neurobiology of this disorder. It offers explanations for many of the challenges faced by individuals with ADHD while also pointing towards potential interventions and areas for further research. As our understanding continues to evolve, it paves the way for more targeted and effective treatments, ultimately improving the lives of adults living with ADHD.

For individuals with ADHD, their families, and healthcare providers, this knowledge can inform better management strategies and foster a more compassionate understanding of the disorder. By recognizing ADHD as a neurobiological condition with its roots in brain function, we can move away from stigmatizing views and toward more effective support and treatment approaches.

As we move forward, integrating our understanding of prefrontal cortex function with broader models of brain network dynamics will be crucial. This holistic approach to understanding ADHD brain function will likely lead to more comprehensive and effective interventions, helping adults with ADHD to manage their symptoms better and achieve their full potential.

Chapter 3
Common Challenges and Misconceptions

Attention-Deficit/Hyperactivity Disorder (ADHD) is a complex neurodevelopmental disorder that affects millions of adults worldwide. Despite increased awareness and research, ADHD remains shrouded in misconceptions and presents unique challenges for those living with the condition. This chapter will explore the common challenges faced by adults with ADHD and debunk prevalent myths surrounding the disorder.

Common Challenges Faced by Adults with ADHD

Living with ADHD as an adult can be a daily struggle, impacting various aspects of life. Understanding these challenges is crucial for developing effective coping strategies and seeking appropriate support.

1. Attention and Focus Issues

One of the most prominent challenges for adults with ADHD is maintaining attention and focus. Dr. Mahendra Perera, in his overview of ADHD challenges, highlights that inattention or the inability to stay focused on a task is a prevalent issue faced by adults with ADHD. This can manifest in several ways:

- Difficulty sustaining attention during tasks, especially those that are not inherently interesting
- Easy distractibility by external stimuli or internal thoughts
- Trouble following through on instructions or completing tasks
- Frequently shifting from one uncompleted activity to another

These attention issues can significantly impact work performance, personal relationships, and overall quality of life. For instance, an adult with ADHD might struggle to complete a work project due to constant distractions, leading to missed deadlines and potential career setbacks.

Dr. Russell Barkley, a leading ADHD researcher, explains, "The ADHD nervous system is interest-based, rather than importance- or priority-based." This means that adults with ADHD often find it challenging to focus on tasks they consider uninteresting, even if these tasks are important.

2. Time Management and Organization

Time management and organization are often significant hurdles for adults with ADHD. According to Medical News Today, individuals with ADHD may experience difficulty predicting how long tasks might take, remembering when certain events happened or are supposed to happen, and ordering events in time. This can lead to:

- Chronic lateness for appointments and meetings
- Missed deadlines at work or school
- Difficulty planning and prioritizing tasks
- Procrastination on important projects
- Feeling overwhelmed by daily responsibilities

These challenges can create a cycle of stress and underachievement as adults with ADHD struggle to meet the time-based demands of work, relationships, and personal life.

Dr. Ari Tuckman, a psychologist specializing in ADHD, notes, "Adults with ADHD often struggle with prospective memory - remembering to remember. This makes it hard to follow through on intentions and commitments."

3. Emotional Regulation

While not officially part of the diagnostic criteria, emotional dysregulation is a common challenge for many adults with ADHD. This can involve:

- Mood swings and irritability
- Difficulty managing frustration and anger
- Heightened emotional reactivity
- Low frustration tolerance
- Rejection sensitivity dysphoria (an intense emotional response to perceived rejection or criticism)

Dr. Vanessa Welch-Pemberton, a psychologist with ADHD, shares her personal experience: "When overstimulated or feeling pressured by multiple demands, I become irritable and snappy." This emotional volatility can strain relationships and create difficulties in professional settings.

Dr. Thomas Brown, another prominent ADHD researcher, explains, "Emotions are an essential part of motivation, organization, and prioritization. When emotions are impaired, as they often are in ADHD, it affects far more than just feelings."

4. Impulsivity and Risk-Taking Behavior

Impulsivity, a core symptom of ADHD, can lead to various challenges in adulthood. Adults with ADHD may struggle with:

- Making hasty decisions without considering the consequences
- Interrupting others in conversation
- Engaging in risky behaviors (e.g., reckless driving, substance abuse)
- Impulsive spending and financial management issues

Dr. Welch-Pemberton notes, "I can be impulsive financially and have a hard time budgeting and saving money, even though I know that good financial management is important." These impulsive tendencies can lead to serious consequences in personal and professional life.

Dr. Ned Hallowell, a psychiatrist with ADHD, describes this impulsivity as "a lack of inhibition, a lack of self-control, or a lack of forethought." He emphasizes that impulsivity can lead to problems, but it can also be a source of spontaneity and creativity when channeled positively.

5. Relationship Difficulties

ADHD can significantly impact personal relationships. WebMD highlights several ways ADHD can complicate social interactions:

- Forgetfulness leading to missed important dates or commitments
- Difficulty listening attentively in conversations
- Impulsive comments that may hurt others' feelings
- Trouble maintaining long-term relationships due to these challenges

These issues can lead to misunderstandings, conflicts, and feelings of rejection or isolation for adults with ADHD.

Dr. Melissa Orlov, an expert on ADHD and relationships, explains, "ADHD symptoms create both emotional and logistical challenges in relationships. Non-ADHD partners often feel ignored or unloved, while the partner with ADHD feels misunderstood and overly criticized."

6. Workplace Challenges

The workplace can be particularly challenging for adults with ADHD. Common issues include:

- Difficulty maintaining focus during long meetings or on complex projects
- Trouble with time management and meeting deadlines
- Disorganization leading to lost documents or missed information
- Struggles with prioritizing tasks and managing workload
- Impulsive decision-making or communication that may impact professional relationships

These challenges can lead to underperformance, job instability, and career dissatisfaction.

Dr. William Dodson, a psychiatrist specializing in ADHD, notes, "The ADHD nervous system is overwhelmed by the many demands of a typical workplace. This can lead to chronic stress and burnout if not properly managed."

7. Academic Struggles

For adults with ADHD pursuing higher education, academic settings can present significant hurdles:

- Difficulty sustaining attention during lectures
- Struggles with long-term projects and time management
- Challenges with organizing study materials and notes
- Test anxiety exacerbated by attention issues
- Procrastination on assignments and studying

These academic challenges can impact educational attainment and future career prospects.

Dr. Patricia Quinn, a developmental pediatrician and ADHD expert, emphasizes, "Many adults with ADHD are highly intelligent but struggle with the executive function demands of higher education. They often benefit from specific learning strategies and accommodations."

8. Low Self-Esteem and Self-Doubt

The cumulative effect of these challenges often leads to low self-esteem and persistent self-doubt. Many adults with ADHD internalize negative feedback and experiences, leading to:

- Feelings of inadequacy or incompetence
- Negative self-talk and self-criticism
- Avoidance of new challenges due to fear of failure
- Imposter syndrome in professional or academic settings

Grace, an individual diagnosed with inattentive ADHD at age 42, shares: "I spend a lot of time in my head and often fail to listen, see, or understand what is important." This internal struggle can significantly impact overall well-being and life satisfaction.

Dr. Sari Solden, a psychotherapist specializing in adult ADHD, explains, "Many adults with ADHD have a lifetime of perceived failures and negative feedback. This can lead to a deep-seated sense of shame and inadequacy that persists even after diagnosis and treatment."

Common Misconceptions About ADHD

Despite increased awareness, many misconceptions about ADHD persist. These myths can lead to stigma, delayed diagnosis, and inadequate support for those with the disorder. Let's examine and debunk some of the most prevalent misconceptions.

1. ADHD Isn't Real

One of the most harmful myths is that ADHD is not a legitimate medical condition. Klarity Health addresses this misconception, stating that

ADHD is often dismissed as a psychiatric label for a natural collection of behaviors. However, extensive research has established ADHD as a genuine neurodevelopmental disorder with biological underpinnings.

Reality: ADHD is recognized by major medical and psychiatric organizations worldwide, including the American Psychiatric Association and the World Health Organization. Neuroimaging studies have shown structural and functional differences in the brains of individuals with ADHD, particularly in areas related to attention, impulse control, and executive function.

Dr. Xavier Castellanos, a prominent ADHD researcher, states, "The evidence for ADHD as a valid disorder is overwhelming. We can see differences in brain structure, function, and connectivity in individuals with ADHD."

2. ADHD Is Just a Childhood Disorder

Many people believe that ADHD is a condition that children "outgrow" as they mature. This misconception can lead to underdiagnosis and a lack of support for adults with ADHD.

Reality: While ADHD is often diagnosed in childhood, it frequently persists into adulthood. "Research suggests that among those children clinically diagnosed with the disorder in childhood, 50-80 percent will continue to meet the criteria for the diagnosis in adolescence, and 10-65 percent may continue to do so in adulthood."

Dr. Joel Young, Medical Director of the Rochester Center for Behavioral Medicine, explains, "ADHD is a lifespan disorder. While some symptoms may change or diminish with age, many adults continue to struggle with ADHD-related challenges throughout their lives."

3. ADHD Is Overdiagnosed

There is a common belief that ADHD is overdiagnosed, particularly in children, leading to unnecessary medication and labeling.

Reality: While diagnostic practices can vary, research does not support the widespread claim of overdiagnosis. Many adults with ADHD, especially women and those with primarily inattentive symptoms, often go undiagnosed for years. The increased recognition of ADHD in recent decades reflects improved diagnostic criteria and greater awareness, not overdiagnosis.

Dr. Stephen Faraone, a leading ADHD researcher, states, "The idea that ADHD is overdiagnosed is not supported by epidemiological data. If anything, ADHD is underdiagnosed in many populations, particularly in adults and females."

4. ADHD Only Affects Boys and Men

The stereotype of ADHD as a disorder primarily affecting hyperactive boys has led to underdiagnosis in girls and women.

Reality: ADHD affects both males and females, although it may present differently. Girls and women are more likely to have inattentive-type ADHD, which may be less noticeable than the hyperactive-impulsive type more common in boys. This difference in presentation can lead to delayed diagnosis or misdiagnosis in females.

Dr. Ellen Littman, a clinical psychologist specializing in gender issues in ADHD, notes, "The historical bias towards studying ADHD in boys has led to a significant under-identification of ADHD in girls and women. This can have serious consequences for their mental health and life outcomes."

5. ADHD Is Caused by Bad Parenting or Too Much Sugar

Some people attribute ADHD symptoms to poor discipline or dietary factors, particularly excessive sugar consumption.

Reality: ADHD is a complex neurodevelopmental disorder with a strong genetic component. While environmental factors can influence symptom expression, they do not cause ADHD. Research has not found a causal link between sugar consumption and ADHD. Good parenting and dietary habits benefit all children but do not prevent or cure ADHD.

Dr. Russell Barkley emphasizes, "ADHD is one of the most heritable psychiatric disorders. While environment plays a role, genetics account for about 75% of the risk for ADHD."

6. People with ADHD Are Just Lazy or Unmotivated

A common misconception is that individuals with ADHD could overcome their symptoms if they tried harder or had more willpower.

Reality: ADHD is a neurobiological disorder that affects executive functions, including motivation and self-regulation. What may appear as laziness is often a struggle with initiating tasks, sustaining attention, and managing time effectively. Many adults with ADHD work extremely hard to compensate for their symptoms and may experience burnout as a result.

Dr. Thomas Brown explains, "ADHD is not a problem of knowing what to do, but of doing what one knows. It's a disorder of performance, not knowledge."

7. ADHD Medications Are Dangerous and Lead to Addiction

There's a widespread concern that ADHD medications, particularly stimulants, are dangerous and lead to substance abuse.

Reality: When used as prescribed under medical supervision, ADHD medications are safe and effective for many individuals. Proper treatment of ADHD, including medication when appropriate, can reduce the risk of substance abuse. Studies have shown that individuals with untreated ADHD are at higher risk for substance use disorders than those receiving appropriate treatment.

Dr. Timothy Wilens, Chief of Child and Adolescent Psychiatry at Massachusetts General Hospital, states, "Long-term studies show that appropriate treatment of ADHD, including medication, reduces the risk of subsequent substance use disorders."

8. Everyone Has a Little ADHD

The idea that everyone experiences ADHD symptoms can sometimes trivialize the struggles of those with the disorder.

Reality: While many people may occasionally experience inattention or restlessness, ADHD involves persistent, pervasive symptoms that significantly impair functioning across multiple areas of life. The intensity, duration, and impact of these symptoms distinguish ADHD from standard variations in attention and behavior.

Dr. Edward Hallowell, a psychiatrist with ADHD, explains, "Saying everyone has a little ADHD is like saying everyone who feels sad is depressed. It minimizes the real struggles of those with the disorder."

9. ADHD Is a Learning Disability

Some people confuse ADHD with learning disabilities, assuming that individuals with ADHD cannot succeed academically.

Reality: While ADHD can impact learning, it is not a learning disability in itself. Many individuals with ADHD are highly intelligent and can excel academically when given appropriate support and accommodations. However, ADHD can co-occur with specific learning disabilities, which may require additional interventions.

Dr. Thomas Brown notes, "ADHD is not a learning disability, but it can significantly interfere with learning. It's a problem with the brain's management system, which can affect various aspects of learning and performance."

10. Adults with ADHD Can't Be Successful

There is a misconception that ADHD inevitably leads to failure in career and personal life.

Reality: Many adults with ADHD lead successful, fulfilling lives. With proper diagnosis, treatment, and support, individuals with ADHD can harness their strengths, such as creativity, hyperfocus, and out-of-the-box thinking. Numerous successful entrepreneurs, artists, and professionals have ADHD and attribute some of their success to the unique way their minds work.

Dr. Ned Hallowell emphasizes, "ADHD can be a gift. Many adults with ADHD are highly creative, intuitive, and able to think outside the box. These qualities can lead to great success when properly channeled."

The Impact of Challenges and Misconceptions

The challenges faced by adults with ADHD, compounded by persistent misconceptions, can significantly impact various aspects of life:

1. Delayed Diagnosis and Treatment

Misconceptions about ADHD can lead to delayed diagnosis, particularly in adults who may have developed coping mechanisms over time. This delay can result in years of unnecessary struggle and missed opportunities for effective treatment.

Dr. David Goodman, Assistant Professor of Psychiatry at Johns Hopkins School of Medicine, states, "Many adults with ADHD go undiagnosed for years, often receiving incorrect diagnoses and ineffective treatments. This can lead to a cascade of personal and professional difficulties."

2. Stigma and Self-Stigma

Societal misunderstandings about ADHD can create stigma, leading to discrimination and social isolation. Additionally, individuals with ADHD may internalize these negative beliefs, leading to self-stigma, low self-esteem, and reluctance to seek help.

Dr. Stephen Hinshaw, a psychologist specializing in ADHD stigma, notes, "The stigma surrounding ADHD can be as damaging as the symptoms themselves. It can prevent individuals from seeking help and lead to internalized shame."

3. Inadequate Support Systems

When ADHD is not properly understood, support systems in schools, workplaces, and communities may be inadequate or inappropriate. This can leave adults with ADHD feeling unsupported and struggling to reach their full potential.

Dr. Patricia Quinn emphasizes, "Proper support can make a world of difference for adults with ADHD. Unfortunately, misconceptions often lead to a lack of appropriate accommodations and understanding."

4. Career and Academic Underachievement

The challenges of ADHD, combined with misconceptions about the disorder, can lead to underachievement in academic and professional settings. This may result in unfulfilled potential and career dissatisfaction.

Dr. Kathleen Nadeau, a clinical psychologist specializing in ADHD, observes, "Many adults with ADHD struggle to reach their full potential in their careers due to a combination of ADHD-related challenges and workplace environments that aren't accommodating to their needs."

5. Relationship Strain

Misunderstandings about ADHD can strain personal relationships. Partners, friends, or family members who don't understand the nature of ADHD may misinterpret symptoms as character flaws or lack of care.

Dr. Melissa Orlov, an expert on ADHD and relationships, notes, "When ADHD is not properly understood in a relationship, it can lead to patterns of frustration, resentment, and misattribution of motives that can seriously damage the connection between partners."

Strategies for Overcoming Challenges and Misconceptions

While the challenges and misconceptions surrounding ADHD can be daunting, adults with ADHD can employ numerous strategies to navigate these difficulties and lead fulfilling lives.

1. Education and Self-Advocacy

One of the most powerful tools for adults with ADHD is education. By thoroughly understanding their condition, individuals can:

- Better explain their needs to others
- Advocate for appropriate accommodations at work or in educational settings
- Recognize and challenge internalized misconceptions

Dr. Russell Barkley emphasizes the importance of self-advocacy: "Adults with ADHD must become experts on their disorder and its management. This knowledge is crucial for effectively communicating needs and navigating various life domains."

2. Developing Personalized Coping Strategies

Every individual with ADHD is unique, and what works for one person may not work for another. Developing personalized coping strategies is crucial. This might include:

- Using digital tools and apps for organization and time management
- Implementing body-doubling techniques for motivation
- Creating structured routines to manage daily tasks
- Utilizing visual aids like mind maps or color-coding systems

Dr. Stephanie Sarkis, an ADHD expert, suggests, "Finding what works for you is a process of trial and error. Be patient with yourself and celebrate small victories. Over time, you'll develop a toolkit of strategies that will help you manage your ADHD effectively."

3. Building a Support Network

Having a strong support network can make a significant difference in managing ADHD. This network might include:

- Family members and friends who understand ADHD
- Support groups for adults with ADHD
- Mental health professionals specializing in ADHD
- Coaches or mentors who can provide guidance and accountability

Dr. Edward Hallowell emphasizes the importance of connection: "Having a support system is crucial for adults with ADHD. It provides emotional support, practical help, and a sense of belonging that can be incredibly empowering."

4. Challenging Stigma and Misconceptions

Actively challenging stigma and misconceptions about ADHD is crucial for creating a more understanding society. This can involve:

- Sharing personal experiences to educate others
- Correcting misinformation when encountered
- Supporting ADHD awareness initiatives and organizations

Dr. Stephen Hinshaw encourages individuals to "turn ADHD into an asset." By highlighting the strengths associated with ADHD, such as creativity and out-of-the-box thinking, individuals can help shift societal perceptions.

5. Seeking Professional Help

Professional help is often crucial in managing ADHD effectively. This may include:

- Working with a psychiatrist for medication management
- Engaging in cognitive-behavioral therapy (CBT) to develop coping skills
- Consulting with an ADHD coach for practical strategies

Dr. Thomas Brown notes, "Comprehensive treatment often involves a combination of medication and behavioral interventions tailored to the individual's needs. Professional guidance can be invaluable in developing an effective treatment plan."

The challenges faced by adults with ADHD are significant and multifaceted, ranging from difficulties with attention and organization to struggles with emotional regulation and self-esteem. These challenges are often compounded by persistent misconceptions about the disorder, which can lead to stigma, delayed diagnosis, and inadequate support.

However, it's essential to recognize that while challenging, ADHD comes with unique strengths and perspectives. Many adults with ADHD possess exceptional creativity, an ability to think outside the box, and a capacity for hyperfocus that can lead to remarkable achievements when properly channeled.

Understanding the realities of ADHD and actively working to dispel myths and misconceptions can create a more supportive and inclusive environment for adults with ADHD. This involves individual efforts and broader societal changes in perceiving and accommodating neurodiversity.

For adults living with ADHD, knowledge is power. Understanding that their struggles are rooted in a neurodevelopmental disorder, not personal failings, can be liberating. It opens the door to seeking appropriate help, developing effective coping strategies, and advocating for necessary accommodations.

As our understanding of ADHD evolves, staying informed and challenging outdated beliefs is essential. By doing so, we can create a world where adults with ADHD are understood, supported, and empowered to reach their full potential.

The journey of living with ADHD may not be easy, but it can be rich with growth, self-discovery, and success. As Dr. Edward Hallowell often says, "Having ADHD is like having a Ferrari engine for a brain, but with bicycle brakes." With the proper support, strategies, and societal understanding, adults with ADHD can learn to harness that powerful engine and navigate life's twists and turns with confidence and skill.

Chapter 4
The Power of Lifestyle Changes

Attention-Deficit/Hyperactivity Disorder (ADHD) is a complex neurodevelopmental disorder that affects millions of adults worldwide. While medication and therapy are often crucial components of ADHD management, the power of lifestyle changes in improving symptoms and overall quality of life cannot be overstated. This chapter will explore various lifestyle modifications that can significantly impact the lives of adults with ADHD.

The Importance of Lifestyle Changes in ADHD Management

Dr. Edward Hallowell, a leading expert in ADHD, emphasizes the significance of lifestyle changes: "Medication can help, but it's not enough. The most effective treatment for ADHD is a combination of medication, when necessary, and lifestyle changes." These changes can help adults with ADHD better manage their symptoms, improve their overall well-being, and enhance their ability to function in various aspects of life.

Diet and Nutrition

The food we consume plays a crucial role in brain function and can significantly impact ADHD symptoms. While there's no specific "ADHD diet," certain dietary approaches have shown promise in managing symptoms.

1. Balanced Nutrition

A well-balanced diet is essential for overall health and can help manage ADHD symptoms. Dr. Uma Naidoo, a nutritional psychiatrist at Harvard Medical School, states, "A diet rich in whole foods, including fruits, vegetables, lean proteins, and healthy fats, can support brain health and potentially alleviate ADHD symptoms."

Essential nutrients that are particularly important for individuals with ADHD include:

- **Omega-3 fatty acids:** These are found in fatty fish, flaxseeds, and walnuts and are crucial for brain function.
- **Iron:** Iron deficiency has been linked to attention problems. Good Iron sources include lean meats and beans.
- **Zinc:** This mineral regulates dopamine. It can be found in oysters, beef, and pumpkin seeds.
- **Magnesium:** Often deficient in individuals with ADHD, magnesium is found in leafy greens, nuts, and whole grains.

2. The Role of Protein

Protein-rich foods can help stabilize blood sugar levels and improve focus. Dr. Hallowell recommends, "Start your day with a protein-rich breakfast. It can help improve concentration and reduce the likelihood of mid-morning energy crashes."

3. Limiting Sugar and Artificial Additives

While sugar doesn't cause ADHD, excessive sugar intake can exacerbate symptoms in some individuals. Dr. Joel Nigg, a psychiatry professor at Oregon Health & Science University, notes, "High sugar intake can lead to blood sugar fluctuations, which may worsen attention and hyperactivity in some people with ADHD."

Similarly, some studies suggest that artificial food colors and preservatives may increase hyperactivity in some children with ADHD. While more research is needed, some adults with ADHD report improvements when avoiding these additives.

4. Caffeine and ADHD

Caffeine, a stimulant, can have varying effects on individuals with ADHD. Dr. John Ratey, associate clinical professor of psychiatry at Harvard Medical School, explains, "For some adults with ADHD, caffeine can improve focus and concentration. However, it's important to be mindful of consumption, as too much can lead to anxiety and sleep problems."

Exercise and Physical Activity

Regular physical activity is one of the most effective lifestyle changes for managing ADHD symptoms. Exercise has been shown to improve attention, reduce impulsivity, and enhance overall cognitive function.

1. The Benefits of Exercise for ADHD

In his book Spark: The Revolutionary New Science of Exercise and the Brain, Dr. John Ratey describes exercise as a "miracle growth for the brain." He explains that physical activity increases the production of neurotransmitters like dopamine and norepinephrine, which are often deficient in individuals with ADHD.

Benefits of regular exercise for adults with ADHD include:

- Improved focus and attention
- Reduced hyperactivity and impulsivity
- Enhanced mood and reduced anxiety
- Better sleep quality
- Increased self-esteem

2. Types of Exercise

Different forms of exercise may offer unique benefits for individuals with ADHD:

- **Aerobic exercise:** Running, cycling, or swimming can improve cardiovascular health and boost brain function.

- **Strength training:** Weightlifting and bodyweight exercises can enhance focus and self-discipline.

- **Yoga and martial arts:** These practices combine physical activity with mindfulness, potentially improving both physical and mental symptoms of ADHD.

Dr. Wendy Suzuki, a neuroscientist at New York University, recommends, "Aim for at least 30 minutes of moderate-intensity exercise most days of the week. Even short bursts of activity throughout the day can be beneficial."

3. Incorporating Movement into Daily Life

Incorporating movement into daily activities can be helpful for adults with ADHD who struggle with traditional exercise routines. Dr. Thomas E. Brown suggests, "Look for opportunities to add physical activity to your day. Take the stairs instead of the elevator, have walking meetings, or use a standing desk."

Sleep Hygiene

Sleep problems are common among adults with ADHD, with many experiencing difficulties falling asleep, staying asleep, or waking up in the morning. Improving sleep hygiene can have a significant impact on ADHD symptoms and overall well-being.

1. The Importance of Sleep for ADHD

Dr. William Dodson, a psychiatrist specializing in ADHD, emphasizes, "Adequate sleep is crucial for cognitive function, emotional regulation, and overall health. For individuals with ADHD, poor sleep can exacerbate symptoms and make managing the disorder more challenging."

2. Strategies for Better Sleep

Implementing good sleep hygiene practices can help improve sleep quality:

- **Maintain a consistent sleep schedule:** Go to bed and wake up simultaneously every day, even on weekends.
- **Create a relaxing bedtime routine:** Engage in calming activities like reading or gentle stretching before bed.
- **Optimize your sleep environment:** Keep your bedroom quiet and cool.
- **Limit screen time before bed:** The blue light emitted by electronic devices can interfere with the production of melatonin, a hormone that regulates sleep.
- **Avoid stimulants in the evening:** Limit caffeine and nicotine intake, especially in the hours before bedtime.

Dr. Russell Barkley suggests, "If racing thoughts keep you awake at night, try keeping a notepad by your bed to jot down any thoughts or worries. This can help clear your mind for sleep."

3. Addressing Sleep Disorders

Some adults with ADHD may have co-occurring sleep disorders that require specific treatment. Dr. Sandra Kooij, a psychiatrist specializing in adult ADHD, notes, "Conditions, like delayed sleep phase syndrome, are common in adults with ADHD and may require interventions such as light therapy or melatonin supplementation under medical supervision."

Stress Management and Mindfulness

Adults with ADHD often experience higher levels of stress and anxiety. Implementing effective stress management techniques and mindfulness practices can help alleviate these issues and improve overall ADHD symptoms.

1. The Impact of Stress on ADHD

Dr. Lidia Zylowska, a psychiatrist and mindfulness expert, explains, "Stress can exacerbate ADHD symptoms, making it harder to focus, regulate emotions, and manage impulses. Learning to manage stress effectively is crucial for adults with ADHD."

2. Mindfulness and Meditation

Mindfulness practices have shown promise in improving attention, reducing impulsivity, and enhancing emotional regulation in adults with ADHD. Dr. Zylowska, author of "The Mindfulness Prescription for Adult ADHD," recommends starting with short, guided meditations and gradually increasing the duration.

Benefits of mindfulness for ADHD include:

- Improved attention and focus

- Reduced emotional reactivity

- Enhanced self-awareness

- Better stress management

3. Other Stress Management Techniques

In addition to mindfulness, other stress management strategies can be beneficial:

- Deep breathing exercises
- Progressive muscle relaxation

- Regular physical activity
- Time in nature
- Engaging in hobbies and creative activities

Dr. Stephanie Sarkis suggests, "Find stress-relief activities that work for you. Some people find coloring or gardening relaxing, while others prefer more active pursuits like sports or dance."

Time Management and Organization

Difficulties with time management and organization are common challenges for adults with ADHD. Implementing effective strategies in these areas can significantly improve daily functioning and reduce stress.

1. The Importance of Structure

Dr. Russell Barkley emphasizes the importance of external structure for individuals with ADHD: "The ADHD brain often struggles with internal motivation and time awareness. Creating external structures and routines can help compensate for these difficulties."

2. Time Management Strategies

Effective time management techniques for adults with ADHD include:

- Using visual timers to increase time awareness
- Breaking tasks into smaller, manageable chunks
- Implementing the "two-minute rule" (if a task takes less than two minutes, do it immediately)
- Utilizing time-blocking techniques to structure the day

Dr. Ari Tuckman recommends, "Experiment with different time management tools and techniques. What works for one person may not work for another. The key is to find strategies that fit your lifestyle and preferences."

3. Organization Tips

Improving organization can help reduce overwhelm and increase productivity:

- Use a planner or digital calendar to keep track of appointments and deadlines
- Implement a "home for everything" system to reduce clutter
- Utilize color coding for files, notes, and calendar entries
- Break larger projects into smaller, actionable steps

Dr. Patricia Quinn suggests, "For adults with ADHD, out of sight often means out of mind. Use visual reminders and open storage systems to keep important items visible and accessible."

Social Connections and Support

Building and maintaining social connections can be challenging for adults with ADHD. Still, social support is crucial for managing the disorder effectively.

1. The Importance of Social Support

Dr. William Dodson notes, "Social support can provide emotional validation, practical assistance, and accountability for adults with ADHD. It's an often overlooked but crucial aspect of ADHD management."

2. Building and Maintaining Relationships

Strategies for improving social connections include:

- Joining ADHD support groups or online communities
- Practicing active listening skills
- Being open about ADHD challenges with trusted friends and family

- Engaging in social activities that align with personal interests

Dr. Hallowell advises, "Don't be afraid to explain your ADHD to close friends and family. Understanding can lead to better support and reduced friction in relationships."

3. Professional Support

Working with professionals who understand ADHD can be invaluable:

- ADHD coaches can help develop personalized strategies for managing symptoms
- Therapists, particularly those specializing in cognitive-behavioral therapy (CBT), can address co-occurring mental health issues and improve coping skills
- Career counselors familiar with ADHD can assist in finding suitable job roles and workplace accommodations

Technology and ADHD Management

While technology can be a source of distraction for individuals with ADHD, it can also be a powerful tool for managing symptoms and improving daily functioning.

1. Productivity Apps

Various apps can help with organization, time management, and focus:

- Task management apps (e.g., Todoist, Trello)
- Time-tracking apps (e.g., RescueTime, Toggl)
- Focus apps that use techniques like the Pomodoro method (e.g., Forest, Focus@Will)

Dr. Tuckman suggests, "Experiment with different apps to find what works best for you. The key is to use technology as a tool to support your goals, not as another source of distraction."

2. Wearable Technology

Smartwatches and fitness trackers can help with time management and health monitoring:

- Set reminders and alarms
- Track sleep patterns
- Monitor physical activity levels

3. Digital Assistants

Voice-activated assistants like Siri, Alexa, or Google Assistant can help with:

- Setting reminders and alarms
- Creating to-do lists
- Quickly looking up information

Dr. Hallowell notes, "Digital assistants can serve as an 'external brain,' helping to offload some of the cognitive demands that can be challenging for individuals with ADHD."

Lifestyle changes can play a crucial role in managing ADHD symptoms and improving the overall quality of life for adults with the disorder. From nutrition and exercise to sleep hygiene and stress management, each aspect of lifestyle modification offers unique benefits.

Dr. Russell Barkley emphasizes, "ADHD is a disorder of performance, not knowledge. Implementing these lifestyle changes consistently is key to seeing improvements."

It's important to remember that there's no one-size-fits-all approach to managing ADHD. What works for one person may not work for another. Dr. Thomas Brown advises, "Be patient with yourself as you experiment with different strategies. It may take time to find the right combination of lifestyle changes that work for you."

Moreover, lifestyle changes should be seen as complementary to, not a replacement for, professional medical advice and treatment. Dr. Patricia Quinn notes, "While lifestyle modifications can be incredibly beneficial, they work best when combined with appropriate medical treatment and therapy as needed."

By embracing these lifestyle changes and working closely with healthcare professionals, adults with ADHD can develop a comprehensive management plan that addresses their unique needs and challenges. Persistence and the right support not only make it possible to manage ADHD symptoms but also to thrive and reach one's full potential.

Remember, managing ADHD is an ongoing journey, and it's okay to adjust your strategies as your needs change. As Dr. Hallowell often says, "Don't just cope with ADHD; learn to thrive with it." With the power of lifestyle changes, that goal is within reach.

Chapter 5
From Awareness to Empowerment

In the first four chapters, we explored the intricate world of ADHD in adults, delving into its neurological basis, common challenges, and the transformative power of lifestyle changes. This foundation sets the stage for actionable strategies that can empower individuals with ADHD to overcome obstacles and thrive. As we transition into Part II, we will shift from understanding ADHD to implementing behavioral strategies for success.

Chapter Summaries: Building a Foundation

1. What is ADHD?

ADHD, or Attention Deficit Hyperactivity Disorder, is often misunderstood as a childhood condition characterized by hyperactivity and inattention. In reality, ADHD persists into adulthood for many individuals, manifesting in diverse ways. Chapter 1 introduced the core symptoms of ADHD—inattention, hyperactivity, and impulsivity—and explained how these traits vary among individuals. By understanding ADHD as a neurological condition rather than a personality flaw, we laid the groundwork for approaching it with compassion and informed strategies.

2. The Adult ADHD Brain: Focus on the Prefrontal Cortex

Chapter 2 explored the science behind ADHD, highlighting the role of the prefrontal cortex in regulating attention, executive function, and emotional control. We explored how differences in brain activity, particularly in dopamine regulation, contribute to the challenges faced by adults with ADHD. This understanding emphasized that ADHD is not a matter of willpower but a neurological difference requiring targeted approaches to manage effectively.

3. Common Challenges and Misconceptions

The third chapter addressed the typical struggles of adults with ADHD, such as difficulties with time management, organization, and emotional regulation. It also tackled pervasive misconceptions, including the idea that ADHD is merely an excuse for laziness or lack of effort. By debunking these myths, we underscored the importance of creating an environment of support and understanding for individuals with ADHD.

4. The Power of Lifestyle Changes

Lifestyle factors like diet, exercise, sleep, and mindfulness are pivotal in managing ADHD symptoms. Chapter 4 explored how adopting healthier routines can enhance focus, mood, and overall well-being. This chapter provided actionable steps for optimizing daily life, from the benefits of regular physical activity to the importance of consistent sleep patterns.

Transitioning to Behavioral Strategies for Success

Understanding ADHD is only the first step. The insights gained from the first four chapters equip us with the knowledge to approach ADHD with empathy and strategy. However, true empowerment comes from turning awareness into action. Part II will guide you through practical, evidence-based behavioral strategies that address the challenges outlined earlier. These strategies will come to life through the stories of Sophia, James, Laura, and Nathan—individuals who have faced ADHD head-on and found ways to thrive.

Each of their journeys highlights a different facet of ADHD management, from building effective routines to improving focus, balancing work and personal life, and enhancing relationships. These real-life examples will inspire and demonstrate how the principles discussed in Part I can be applied in various contexts.

Preparing for What's Next

As we move into Part II, remember that every individual's experience with ADHD is unique. The strategies that worked for Sophia, James, Laura, and Nathan may need to be tailored to fit your circumstances. The key is approaching this process with curiosity, patience, and a willingness to experiment.

In the upcoming chapters, we will explore how cognitive and behavioral strategies can transform ADHD challenges into opportunities for growth. Combining the foundational knowledge from Part I with the actionable tools in Part II will equip you to create a life that celebrates your strengths and supports your needs.

Let's take the next step together, moving from awareness to empowerment, and embark on a journey of self-discovery, growth, and success.

Part II:
Behavioral Strategies for Success

Chapter 6

Sophia's Story

As we transition into Part II: Behavioral Strategies for Success, we delve into the heart of creating lasting change. We will now focus on applying cognitive behavioral strategies to address the specific challenges that Sophia, James, Laura, and Nathan face.

Each of these individuals represents a unique ADHD journey, from the academic pressures of college life to the professional and personal balancing act of adulthood. Through their stories, you will witness how targeted strategies can transform procrastination into productivity, chaos into clarity, and self-doubt into confidence. This section will provide insights into their progress and offer actionable techniques to apply to your life. Let their transformations inspire you to embrace the possibility of rewiring your brain for better focus, productivity, and success.

Sophia Martinez, a bright and ambitious 20-year-old college student, seemed to have it all figured out when she first set foot on campus. Growing up in a suburban neighborhood, Sophia's parents often described her as "full of potential" but "always scattered." They watched as their youngest child excelled in activities she loved, like theater and art, but struggled to stay consistent in academics. Sophia's teachers praised her creativity yet expressed concern over her frequent forgetfulness, incomplete assignments, and inability to stay organized. Diagnosed with ADHD at 15, Sophia briefly attended therapy and tried medication, but once she finished high school, she felt she could handle things on her own. College, however, presented an entirely new set of challenges.

The Promise of a Fresh Start

Sophia had always dreamed of attending university, believing it would be a fresh start and a chance to achieve her goals finally. Majoring in Psychology, she was fascinated by human behavior and motivated by a desire to help others navigate their struggles. Yet, as the semesters progressed, Sophia's enthusiasm dimmed under the weight of her ADHD symptoms. The structured environment of high school had given way to the uncharted territory of college life, where time management and self-discipline were critical. For someone with ADHD, this lack of structure was both liberating and paralyzing.

Struggles with Time Management

One of Sophia's biggest challenges was managing her time effectively. She often felt overwhelmed by her workload, especially when assignments piled up. Instead of starting early, Sophia would procrastinate until the night before a deadline, consumed by anxiety and regret. Her dorm room became a familiar scene of late-night cramming sessions, littered with empty coffee cups and scattered notes. Despite her best efforts, she often missed key details or failed to fully grasp the material, leading to lower grades than she had hoped for. This cycle of procrastination and underperformance left Sophia feeling increasingly defeated.

Challenges with Focus and Organization

In addition to academic struggles, Sophia found it challenging to stay focused during lectures. Her professors' voices often faded into background noise as her mind wandered to unrelated thoughts. She would furiously jot down notes in an attempt to stay engaged, but upon reviewing them later, the notes rarely made sense. Group projects were another source of stress. Sophia's tendency to forget deadlines or misplace important materials made her feel like a liability to her peers. She began to dread collaborative assignments, worried that her ADHD would disappoint others.

Organization was another uphill battle. Sophia's planner—a gift from her mom meant to keep her on track—sat largely unused at the bottom of her backpack. Her desk was a chaotic jumble of books, papers, and supplies, making it nearly impossible to find what she needed when she needed it. This disorganization extended beyond her academics into her personal life. She frequently lost her keys, wallet, and even her phone, adding unnecessary stress to her already hectic days. Friends teased her about being "scatterbrained," but Sophia often felt ashamed and frustrated with herself.

The Social and Emotional Toll

Socially, Sophia's ADHD created additional challenges. While she was friendly and outgoing, her tendency to cancel plans at the last minute—usually to catch up on neglected schoolwork—strained her relationships. Her friends grew tired of her unreliability, and Sophia began isolating herself, believing she could not maintain meaningful connections. She longed for close friendships but worried that her ADHD made her too "much" for others to handle.

The emotional toll of these struggles was profound. Sophia often felt like she was falling short in every aspect of her life, from academics to relationships. Her self-esteem plummeted as she compared herself to her peers, who easily navigated college. Anxiety became a constant companion, whispering doubts about her ability to succeed. Sophia began to question whether she was even cut out for college. The pressure to meet expectations—both her own and those of her family—weighed heavily on her, amplifying her feelings of inadequacy.

Misunderstandings and the Need for Support

Sophia's parents, though supportive, didn't fully understand the challenges she faced. They encouraged her to "just focus" or "try harder," unaware that ADHD made these tasks infinitely more difficult. While they meant well, their advice often left Sophia feeling misunderstood and alone. She wanted to explain what it was like to live with ADHD but struggled to articulate the invisible barriers she faced daily. This lack of understanding extended to her professors, who sometimes dismissed her requests for accommodations as excuses.

A Turning Point

Despite these difficulties, Sophia refused to give up on her dreams. She knew she was capable of more and was determined to find a way to manage her ADHD effectively. Her decision to seek help marked a turning point in her journey. Encouraged by a friend, Sophia began working with an ADHD coach, who introduced her to cognitive-behavioral strategies designed specifically for individuals with ADHD. She also started using tools like digital planners and apps to keep track of her assignments and deadlines. These small steps gave her a sense of control and hope that change was possible.

Inspiration Through Resilience

Sophia's story is a testament to the resilience and determination of individuals with ADHD. Her struggles are not unique; many college students face similar challenges as they navigate the demands of higher education. Yet, Sophia's willingness to confront these obstacles head-on with the help of her ADHD coach makes her journey an inspiring example of what's possible with the right tools and mindset. In this chapter, we will follow Sophia as she implements cognitive-behavioral strategies to tackle her ADHD symptoms over the next 90 days. From mastering time management to improving focus and organization, Sophia's progress will offer valuable insights for anyone looking to rewrite their ADHD story.

Chapter 7

A New Beginning with an ADHD Coach

Deciding to meet with an ADHD coach was not an easy decision for Sophia Martinez. She had wrestled with self-doubt for weeks, uncertain if seeking help would make any difference. Encouraged by her friend, who had seen significant improvements in her life with coaching, Sophia finally decided it was worth a try. She entered the coach's office with hope and apprehension, clutching a notebook filled with questions she hoped would steer the conversation.

The coach, Amanda Carter, welcomed Sophia warmly and quickly put her at ease. Coach Carter had been working with individuals with ADHD for over a decade and specialized in helping college students navigate their unique challenges. Her office was a calm and organized space, reflecting the strategies she taught her clients. A whiteboard covered in diagrams and motivational quotes dominated one wall. A small table held various tools: planners, timers, and colorful sticky notes—simple but effective aids for managing ADHD symptoms.

Ms. Carter began the session by asking Sophia about her background, challenges, and what she hoped to achieve through coaching. Sophia, though initially hesitant, found herself opening up about her struggles with procrastination, poor time management, and a constant sense of being overwhelmed. She spoke about her difficulties staying focused during lectures, her disorganization, and how these issues impacted her self-esteem and relationships.

Ms. Carter listened attentively, jotting down notes and occasionally nodding in understanding. When Sophia finished, she smiled reassuringly. "You've already taken a huge step by being here," Ms. Carter said. "The challenges you're facing are common for individuals with ADHD, but the good news is that there are strategies we can implement to help you manage them effectively."

The Assessment

The first step in Ms. Carter's process was a comprehensive assessment of Sophia's current habits, routines, and areas of difficulty. She asked Sophia to describe a typical day in her life, probing for details about how she spent her time, where she felt most productive, and where she encountered obstacles. Sophia described her mornings as chaotic, often oversleeping and rushing to get to class. Her afternoons were unstructured, with time slipping away as she attempted to study but got distracted by her phone, social media, or daydreams. Evenings were a frantic attempt to catch up on everything she hadn't accomplished earlier in the day.

Ms. Carter also explored Sophia's strengths. "What are the things you feel you're really good at or enjoy doing?" she asked. Sophia's face lit up as she talked about her love for art and how she could spend hours painting or sketching without losing focus. Ms. Carter noted this down, recognizing that harnessing Sophia's passions could be an essential part of her plan.

To gain further insight, Ms. Carter asked Sophia to complete a self-assessment questionnaire designed to identify patterns in her behavior. The results confirmed what Sophia had shared: she struggled most with time management, staying focused on tasks, and organizing her environment. The questionnaire also revealed that anxiety played a significant role in exacerbating her symptoms, creating a cycle of procrastination and self-doubt.

Developing the Coaching Plan

On completing the assessment, Ms. Carter outlined a coaching plan tailored to Sophia's needs. "Our goal is to help you build systems that work for your brain," she explained. "This isn't about trying to change who you are but about finding strategies that align with your strengths and help you overcome your challenges."

1. Building a Structured Routine

Ms. Carter suggested starting with a structured daily routine. She explained that people with ADHD often thrive with consistency and clear expectations. Together, they worked on creating a realistic schedule for Sophia's weekdays. The plan included setting times for waking up, attending classes, studying, eating, exercising, and relaxing. Ms. Carter emphasized the importance of incorporating breaks to prevent burnout and suggested using alarms and reminders to stay on track.

"The key is to start small," she advised. "We're not aiming for perfection. Even sticking to this schedule 70% of the time will make a significant difference."

2. Time Management Tools

Next, Ms. Carter introduced Sophia to time management tools such as digital planners and time-blocking techniques. She recommended using a planner app that allowed Sophia to schedule tasks and set reminders. They practiced breaking down large assignments into smaller, manageable steps and assigning deadlines for each step. "This will help reduce the feeling of being overwhelmed," Ms. Carter explained. "When tasks are smaller, they're easier to tackle."

Ms. Carter also encouraged Sophia to experiment with the Pomodoro Technique, which involves working for 25 minutes followed by a 5-minute break. "This method can help you stay focused while also giving your brain the rest it needs," she said.

3. Organization Strategies

Recognizing Sophia's struggles with disorganization, Ms. Carter proposed decluttering her physical and digital spaces. They discussed dedicating a weekend to reorganizing her dorm room and creating designated spots for important items like keys and school supplies. Coach Carter suggested using color-coded folders for her class materials and creating a digital filing system for her notes and assignments.

"A clear space leads to a clearer mind," Dr. Carter said. "It may feel overwhelming at first, but we'll tackle it step by step."

4. Addressing Anxiety

Since anxiety was a significant factor in Sophia's struggles, Ms. Carter incorporated mindfulness exercises into the plan. She taught Sophia simple breathing techniques to use when she felt overwhelmed and recommended journaling as a way to process her emotions. "Mindfulness can help you stay grounded and reduce the spiral of negative thoughts," she explained.

5. Leveraging Strengths

Finally, Ms. Carter emphasized the importance of leveraging Sophia's strengths and passions. They brainstormed ways to incorporate art into her study routines, such as using visual aids like mind maps or doodling key concepts to reinforce learning. "Your creativity is one of your greatest assets," Ms. Carter said. "Let's find ways to use it to your advantage."

The Path Forward

As the session came to a close, Sophia felt a sense of relief and optimism she hadn't experienced in months. For the first time in years, she had a clear plan tailored to her unique needs and challenges. Ms. Carter provided her with a list of action items to work on before their next meeting and reminded her to be patient with herself.

"Progress takes time," Ms. Carter said. "There will be setbacks, but each step you take brings you closer to where you want to be."

Sophia left the office that day with a renewed sense of purpose. She knew the road ahead wouldn't be easy, but she felt empowered to take control of her life and work toward her goals. The coaching plan was not just a set of strategies; it was a roadmap to a better future, one that honored her strengths and addressed her challenges head-on.

Chapter 8
Empowering Change Through Cognitive Behavioral Strategies

Sophia Martinez felt hopeful when she walked away from her first session with Coach Carter. For the first time in years, she had a clear roadmap to address the challenges caused by her ADHD. What stood out to her most during their meeting was how Coach Carter used cognitive behavioral strategies to break down overwhelming problems into manageable solutions. These strategies would serve as the foundation for Sophia's transformation in three critical areas: developing a structured routine, creating practical time management tools, and becoming more organized.

Developing a Structured Routine

For Sophia, mornings had always been chaotic. Oversleeping, skipping breakfast, and rushing to class had become the norm, setting a frantic tone for the rest of her day. Coach Carter explained that establishing a structured routine could alleviate much of this stress by introducing predictability and reducing decision fatigue. Using cognitive behavioral strategies, Sophia and Coach Carter identified the barriers preventing her from sticking to a routine and designed a system tailored to her needs.

First, Coach Carter asked Sophia to keep a journal for one week, recording how she spent her time each day. This exercise served two purposes: it helped Sophia identify where she was losing time and brought awareness to procrastination patterns. Reviewing the journal, they noticed that Sophia often stayed up late scrolling through social media, making it difficult to wake up on time. This lack of sleep spilled over into her mornings, creating a domino effect that disrupted her entire day.

Using this insight, Coach Carter guided Sophia in creating a morning and evening routine. For her evenings, they implemented a "wind-down" period that included setting an alarm for 10:00 PM to signal it was time to disconnect from her phone and prepare for bed. They built a simple checklist to make mornings less overwhelming: wake up at 7:30 AM, drink water, make her bed, and eat breakfast. Each task was small and achievable, giving Sophia a sense of accomplishment before starting her day.

Coach Carter also introduced the concept of "habit stacking," a cognitive behavioral strategy where new habits are linked to existing ones. For example, Sophia reviewed her planner during breakfast, combining a familiar routine with a new productive habit. Anchoring these tasks to specific times and activities made it easier for Sophia to stick to her schedule.

Creating Effective Time Management Tools

Sophia's time management struggles were among the most significant barriers to her academic success. She often underestimated how long tasks would take, leading to late submissions and last-minute cramming sessions. Coach Carter introduced several cognitive behavioral strategies to help Sophia control her time.

The first step was understanding Sophia's perception of time. People with ADHD often experience what Coach Carter called "time blindness," where they have difficulty gauging how long tasks will take or prioritizing deadlines. Coach Carter suggested using a visual timer during study sessions to combat this. The timer allowed Sophia to see the passage of time, helping her stay focused and aware of how long she had been working.

Next, they practiced breaking down large assignments into smaller, more manageable steps—a cognitive strategy called "task chunking." For example, instead of writing an entire research paper in one sitting, Sophia divided the project into stages: researching sources, creating an outline, drafting, and editing. Each stage was assigned a specific day and time, making the overall task feel less daunting.

Coach Carter also introduced Sophia to the Pomodoro Technique, a popular time management tool that aligns well with cognitive behavioral principles. The technique involves working for 25 minutes, followed by a 5-minute break. This approach appealed to Sophia because it created a sense of urgency and provided regular opportunities to recharge. She began using a Pomodoro timer during her study sessions, finding that the structure helped her stay focused and productive.

Additionally, Sophia learned the importance of prioritization. Coach Carter helped her categorize tasks using the Eisenhower Matrix, a tool that divides tasks into four quadrants based on urgency and importance. This strategy allowed Sophia to focus on high-priority tasks first while delegating or delaying less critical ones. By applying this system, Sophia could manage her workload more efficiently and reduce feeling overwhelmed.

Becoming More Organized

Disorganization had long been a source of frustration for Sophia. Her cluttered dorm room and scattered notes made it difficult to find what she needed when she needed it. Coach Carter emphasized that becoming organized was not about perfection but about creating systems that worked for Sophia's unique brain.

They started with Sophia's physical space. Using cognitive behavioral techniques, Coach Carter encouraged Sophia to visualize what an organized space would look like and how it would make her feel. This mental exercise helped Sophia connect the task of decluttering with positive emotions, motivating her to take action. Together, they created a step-by-step plan for tackling her dorm room, one small area at a time.

Coach Carter introduced the "one-minute rule," a simple strategy where Sophia committed to completing any task that took less than one minute, such as putting away her shoes or filing a paper. This rule helped Sophia build momentum and prevented small tasks from piling up into overwhelming messes.

Coach Carter recommended organizing her class materials into folders on her laptop to address her digital clutter. Each class had its own folder with subcategories for notes, assignments, and readings. This system made it easier for Sophia to locate files quickly and reduced the time she spent searching for misplaced documents.

Coach Carter also introduced tools such as color-coded binders and sticky notes to support Sophia's organization efforts. Visual cues like these helped Sophia differentiate between tasks and prioritize her work. They also discussed the importance of conducting a weekly "reset," where Sophia would review her planner, tidy her workspace, and prepare for the week ahead. This ritual gave Sophia a sense of control and allowed her to start each week with a clean slate.

The Impact of Cognitive Behavioral Strategies

As Sophia implemented these cognitive behavioral strategies, she began to notice significant changes in her daily life. Her structured routine provided a sense of stability and helped her approach each day intentionally. The time management tools reduced her procrastination and allowed her to stay on top of her assignments without feeling overwhelmed. Meanwhile, her newfound organizational skills made her environment less stressful and more conducive to productivity.

Perhaps most importantly, these strategies helped Sophia build confidence in managing her ADHD. Each small success reinforced her belief that she could change her life positively. While challenges still arose, Sophia now had a toolkit of strategies to address them head-on.

Coach Carter's guidance and applying cognitive behavioral strategies marked a turning point in Sophia's journey. By systematically addressing her ADHD symptoms, Sophia learned how to work with her brain rather than against it. Her progress was a testament to the power of tailored strategies and the resilience of the human spirit.

Chapter 9

Sophia's Journey to Mastery

Sophia Martinez knew that implementing the cognitive behavioral strategies Coach Carter had taught her was only the first step. The true challenge was consistently practicing these strategies in her daily life. Over the next few weeks, Sophia embarked on a journey of trial and error, applying the tools she had learned to her routines, time management, and organization. Along the way, she faced a significant setback that tested her resilience but ultimately strengthened her commitment to change.

Week 1: Building the Foundation

Sophia began her journey by focusing on her structured routine. She set her alarm for 7:30 AM and placed her phone on the other side of the room to force herself to get out of bed. Her evenings now ended with a 10:00 PM reminder to start her wind-down routine, which included laying out clothes for the next day, reviewing her planner, and reading a book instead of scrolling through her phone. These small changes made her mornings feel more manageable and less rushed.

To reinforce her new habits, Sophia used habit stacking. For instance, she paired brushing her teeth with glancing at her checklist of morning tasks. This combination of physical and mental preparation gave her a sense of accomplishment before heading to class.

By the end of the first week, Sophia was feeling optimistic. Though not every day had gone perfectly, she noticed that her mornings were less chaotic and her focus during lectures had slightly improved. She began to trust the process and believed that these strategies could make a lasting impact.

Week 2: Tackling Time Management

In the second week, Sophia shifted her focus to mastering the Pomodoro Technique and task chunking. She used a timer app on her phone to break her study sessions into 25-minute blocks, with short breaks in between. The timer helped her stay on track during study periods, and she found the breaks refreshing. During these breaks, she stretched, drank water, or stepped outside for fresh air, which prevented mental fatigue.

Sophia also started breaking down her assignments into smaller tasks. She created a timeline for a history essay due in three weeks: Week 1 for research, Week 2 for drafting, and Week 3 for revisions. This approach prevented her from feeling overwhelmed and gave her a clear sense of progress.

One challenge Sophia faced was underestimating how long tasks would take. She often found herself running out of time during her Pomodoro sessions. Coach Carter had warned her about this common issue, so Sophia began keeping track of how long specific tasks took. Over time, this helped her improve her ability to plan realistically.

Week 3: Organizing Her Environment

Week three was all about decluttering and creating organizational systems. Sophia dedicated a Saturday afternoon to cleaning her dorm room. She tackled one area at a time, starting with her desk. Using Coach Carter's one-minute rule, she quickly sorted through papers and put away small items. She followed the task chunking strategy for larger tasks, like organizing her textbooks and notebooks and spreading the work over two days.

Sophia also implemented a digital organization system for her laptop. She created folders for each class, with subfolders for notes, assignments, and resources. She color-coded her folders and renamed files with clear labels to make accessing her materials easier. By the end of the week, Sophia's workspace felt less overwhelming, and she noticed she could find whatever she needed significantly faster.

Sophia scheduled a weekly reset every Sunday evening to maintain this new level of organization. During this time, she reviewed her planner, tidied her space, and mentally prepared for the upcoming week. This routine gave her a sense of control and allowed her to start each week with clarity.

The Setback

Despite her progress, Sophia faced a significant setback during the fourth week. With midterms approaching, she felt the familiar pressure to perform well. Old habits resurfaced as she procrastinated studying for her biology exam, convincing herself she still had plenty of time. When the exam date arrived, Sophia realized she had barely prepared. The test was a disaster, and she left the classroom feeling defeated.

This failure triggered a spiral of negative thoughts. Sophia began doubting her ability to succeed and questioned whether all her efforts had been in vain. That night, she skipped her evening routine, reverting to mindlessly scrolling through her phone and ignoring her planner. The following day, she overslept and missed her first class, amplifying her feelings of inadequacy.

Bouncing Back

After a few days of self-doubt, Sophia reached out to Coach Carter. During their session, she tearfully explained her setback and expressed frustration at her perceived lack of progress. Coach Carter listened empathetically and reminded Sophia that setbacks were a natural part of any growth process.

"What matters is not that you stumbled," Coach Carter said, "but how you choose to move forward. Let's take this as an opportunity to learn." Together, they analyzed what had gone wrong. They identified that Sophia's procrastination stemmed from her anxiety about the biology exam's difficulty and fear of failure. This avoidance had created a vicious cycle that left her unprepared.

To address this, Coach Carter introduced Sophia to a new strategy: reframing her mindset about challenges. Instead of viewing exams as high-stakes tests of her worth, she practiced seeing them as opportunities to demonstrate her knowledge. They also discussed recognizing early signs of avoidance and implementing counterstrategies, such as starting with smaller, less intimidating study tasks.

Sophia left the session feeling reassured and refocused. She revisited her routines and committed to preparing for her upcoming exams more intentionally. This time, she started studying earlier, used her Pomodoro timer to break study sessions into manageable chunks, and reviewed her progress each evening.

Building Resilience

The experience taught Sophia an essential lesson about resilience. She realized that setbacks were opportunities to grow stronger, not erasing her progress. By facing her challenges head-on and using Coach Carter's tools, Sophia regained her confidence and built a deeper understanding of her ADHD.

In the weeks that followed, Sophia continued to refine her strategies. She added a "self-check-in" to her weekly reset, where she reflected on what had gone well and what needed improvement. This practice helped her stay accountable and adapt to new challenges.

Sophia's journey was far from perfect, but it was undeniably transformative. The combination of cognitive behavioral strategies, persistence, and support from Coach Carter enabled her to navigate the ups and downs of her ADHD with greater clarity and control. Through her determination, Sophia discovered that growth is not a straight path but a series of steps forward, backward, and ultimately upward.

Chapter 10

James' Story

James Carter sat in his car, gripping the steering wheel tightly as the city buzzed around him. It had been another exhausting day at the tech startup where he worked as a project manager. At 34, James often felt like he was drowning in a sea of responsibilities, struggling to keep his head above water. He was a creative thinker, a problem solver, and someone who could see solutions where others could not. Yet, despite these strengths, James often found himself overwhelmed by the sheer volume of tasks he needed to juggle. Deadlines slipped, details were missed, and his team—though patient—had started expressing frustration with his inconsistency. For James, the underlying cause of his struggles was clear: ADHD.

James had been diagnosed with ADHD as a child. His parents, supportive but unsure of how to help, had tried therapy and medication during his early years. While these interventions provided some relief, James' symptoms persisted into adulthood. By the time he reached his 20s, he decided to stop treatment, believing he could manage on his own. For a while, he succeeded. His creativity and out-of-the-box thinking allowed him to excel in jobs that valued innovation. However, as his career advanced and the demands of his role increased, the cracks in his coping mechanisms began to show.

The High-Stakes Environment

As a project manager at a fast-paced tech startup, James thrived on the creative aspects of his role. He loved brainstorming new ideas, collaborating with developers, and envisioning the bigger picture. However, the administrative and logistical tasks that came with managing multiple projects often left him feeling drained and scattered. James struggled to prioritize tasks, frequently switching between projects without completing them. This lack of follow-through frustrated his colleagues, who relied on him to provide direction and ensure deadlines were met.

One of James' biggest challenges was staying focused during team meetings. James' mind often wandered while his colleagues discussed project timelines and technical details. He found it challenging to stay engaged with topics that did not immediately capture his interest. At times, he would interrupt with tangential ideas or questions, unintentionally derailing the conversation. Though his team appreciated his enthusiasm and creativity, they sometimes grew impatient with his inability to stay on topic.

The Cycle of Overwhelm

James' difficulties with organization and time management created a cycle of overwhelm that felt impossible to break. His email inbox was perpetually overflowing, with essential messages buried under a mountain of unread notifications. He often missed deadlines or responded to requests too late, causing delays in project timelines. James would work long hours to compensate for these lapses, often staying late at the office or bringing work home. These extended hours left him exhausted and irritable, further impacting his performance.

This cycle of overwhelm spilled into James' personal life. At home, his wife often expressed frustration with his forgetfulness and lack of follow-through on household responsibilities. Bills went unpaid, groceries were forgotten, and clutter piled up in their shared living space. Though James wanted to be more reliable, he felt paralyzed by the sheer volume of tasks vying for his attention. He often felt like a failure, unable to live up to the expectations of those around him.

The Emotional Toll

The challenges James faced at work and home took a significant emotional toll on him. He often experienced feelings of guilt and shame, believing he was letting down his team and his partner. These emotions were compounded by the stigma surrounding ADHD in adults, which left James feeling isolated and misunderstood. He avoided discussing his struggles with colleagues, worried they might perceive him as incompetent or unreliable.

Anxiety became a constant companion, amplifying his ADHD symptoms and creating a vicious cycle. When faced with a daunting task or looming deadline, James would procrastinate, seeking temporary relief from his stress. But as the deadline approached, the anxiety would return, magnified by the knowledge that he had put off the task. This pattern left James feeling trapped, unable to break free from the grip of his ADHD.

Seeking Help

After months of grappling with these challenges, James reached a breaking point. A particularly stressful week at work culminated in a missed deadline that cost his team an important client. Though his colleagues were supportive, James could see their frustration and disappointment. That evening, his wife confronted him about their mounting household responsibilities, expressing resentment and exhaustion. For James, it was a wake-up call. He realized he could not continue living this way and sought help.

Encouraged by his wife, James began researching ADHD coaching and cognitive behavioral strategies. He was skeptical at first, worried that these approaches might not address the unique challenges he faced as an adult with ADHD. But after reading testimonials from others who had benefited from coaching, James decided to try it. He contacted a coach who specialized in working with professionals and scheduled his first session.

The Turning Point

James' decision to seek help marked a turning point in his journey. During his initial session, his coach helped him identify the specific areas where his ADHD was impacting his life the most. Together, they developed a plan to address his organization, time management, and focus struggles. James felt hope as he left the session, armed with practical tools and strategies to tackle his challenges.

Over the following weeks, James began implementing these strategies with the guidance of his coach. He started using a digital planner to track his tasks and deadlines, breaking down larger projects into smaller, manageable steps. He practiced mindfulness techniques to stay focused during meetings and used a notebook to jot down key points and reminders. At home, he and his partner created a shared chore chart to divide responsibilities more equitably.

Though the journey was not without setbacks, James began seeing significant improvements in his professional and personal life. He discovered that small, consistent changes could have a profound impact, and he felt a renewed sense of confidence in his ability to manage his ADHD. Most importantly, he realized that seeking help was not a sign of weakness but a courageous step toward living a more fulfilling life.

Moving Forward

James' story is a testament to the resilience and determination of adults with ADHD. His challenges were not unique, but his willingness to confront them head-on and seek support set him apart. Through coaching and cognitive behavioral strategies, James learned how to harness his strengths and navigate his ADHD with greater clarity and control.

In this chapter, we will explore James' journey in greater detail, highlighting his strategies to overcome his struggles and the lessons he learned along the way. His story serves as a reminder that, with the right tools and support, individuals with ADHD can thrive in even the most demanding environments. James' experience offers hope and inspiration to anyone facing similar challenges, proving that it's never too late to take charge of your life.

Chapter 11

A New Strategy for Success

James Carter walked into his first meeting with his ADHD coach feeling hopeful and skeptical. His wife had encouraged him to seek help, and though James recognized that he needed support, he was not sure what to expect. Would coaching address the challenges he faced every day at work and home? Could it provide him with the tools to manage his overwhelming responsibilities?

The coach, Michael Bennett, greeted James with a firm handshake and a warm smile. Coach Bennett had worked with adults managing ADHD for over a decade and specialized in helping professionals find balance and productivity in their careers and personal lives. His office was welcoming. It has a whiteboard covered in diagrams and notes from recent sessions, shelves of neatly organized books, and a small table holding various tools like planners, timers, and sticky notes.

"I'm glad you're here, James," Coach Bennett said as they sat down. "ADHD is a challenge, but it's not a roadblock. With the right strategies, we can turn your challenges into opportunities. Let's start by talking about what brought you here and what you hope to achieve."

The Assessment

James began by describing his struggles at work. He explained how he often felt overwhelmed by his responsibilities as a project manager at a tech startup, where he needed to juggle multiple projects, coordinate with teams, and meet tight deadlines. His inability to prioritize tasks and stay focused during meetings created friction with his colleagues, and he frequently worked late to make up for lost time.

James' ADHD had also taken a toll at home. His wife often expressed frustration with his forgetfulness and lack of follow-through on household responsibilities. Bills were sometimes paid late, chores went undone, and James' disorganization frequently derailed plans. Though he wanted to be a reliable husband, James felt trapped in a cycle of procrastination and guilt.

Coach Bennett listened attentively, occasionally asking clarifying questions or jotting down notes. Once James had finished, the coach outlined the next step: a comprehensive assessment of James' current habits and routines. "To create a coaching plan that works for you," Coach Bennett explained, "we need to identify where your ADHD is impacting your life most and figure out how to address those areas systematically."

The assessment involved several components. First, James completed a self-evaluation questionnaire designed to highlight patterns in his behavior, such as how he approached tasks, managed time, and responded to stress. Next, Coach Bennett asked James to describe a typical day in detail, from morning routines to how he spent his evenings. They also discussed James' strengths—his creativity, problem-solving skills, and ability to think outside the box—and his stress and procrastination triggers.

By the end of the assessment, several key themes had emerged. James struggled most with prioritization, task management, and staying focused in both work and personal settings. Anxiety often exacerbated his symptoms, creating a cycle of avoidance and self-criticism. However, his strengths as a creative thinker and natural leader provided a solid foundation for growth.

Developing the Coaching Plan

With the assessment complete, Coach Bennett outlined a coaching plan tailored to James' needs. "This plan is a starting point," he explained.

"We'll adjust as we go, based on what works and what doesn't. The goal is to build systems that align with your strengths and address your challenges in manageable steps."

1. Prioritization and Task Management

The first focus area was helping James prioritize his tasks effectively. Coach Bennett introduced him to the Eisenhower Matrix, a tool for categorizing tasks based on their urgency and importance. Together, they practiced sorting James' to-do list into four quadrants:

- **Urgent and Important:** Tasks requiring immediate attention, such as critical work deadlines.

- **Important but Not Urgent:** Long-term goals and projects, like career development tasks.

- **Urgent but Not Important:** Tasks that could be delegated or addressed quickly.

- **Neither Urgent nor Important:** Low-priority distractions to minimize or eliminate.

This exercise helped James recognize where he was spending unnecessary energy and refocus on what mattered most. To further support his task management, Coach Bennett suggested using a digital task manager app that allowed James to set deadlines, reminders, and priorities for each task.

2. Creating Structure and Routine

Recognizing that James' days often lacked structure, Coach Bennett emphasized the importance of creating consistent routines. Together, they designed a daily schedule that balanced work, family time, and self-care. Mornings began with a 15-minute planning session, during which James would review his daily tasks and set specific goals. Evenings included a wind-down routine to help him transition from work mode to relaxation.

Coach Bennett also recommended time-blocking—allocating specific periods for focused work on individual projects. This strategy allowed James to concentrate on one task at a time, reducing the distractions that often derailed his productivity. To make time-blocking more effective, they incorporated the Pomodoro Technique, breaking work sessions into 25-minute intervals with 5-minute breaks in between.

3. Enhancing Focus and Minimizing Distractions

Coach Bennett introduced strategies to reduce distractions and address James' difficulty staying focused during meetings and work sessions. These included:

- **Setting Boundaries:** Turning off email and app notifications during focused work periods.

- **Using Visual Cues:** Keeping a notebook handy to jot down unrelated thoughts or ideas that popped up, allowing James to stay on track.

- **Mindfulness Techniques:** Practicing deep breathing exercises before meetings to calm his mind and increase attention.

Coach Bennett also suggested that James request a weekly one-on-one meeting with his supervisor to review priorities and ensure alignment on project timelines. This proactive approach helped James stay organized and improved communication with his team.

4. Managing Stress and Building Resilience

Since anxiety played a significant role in James' challenges, Coach Bennett incorporated stress management techniques into the plan. These included journaling to process emotions, practicing gratitude to shift focus from negative to positive thoughts, and engaging in physical activity to release built-up tension.

Additionally, they worked on reframing James' mindset about mistakes. Instead of viewing setbacks as failures, James considered them learning opportunities. This shift in perspective helped reduce the self-criticism that often paralyzed him.

5. Strengthening Communication and Relationships

To improve his relationship with his wife, James, and Coach Bennett developed strategies for better communication. These included scheduling regular check-ins to discuss household responsibilities and using shared digital tools to coordinate tasks and deadlines. James also committed to expressing appreciation for his wife's support and acknowledging her efforts.

The Path Forward

As their session ended, James felt a sense of relief and optimism. The coaching plan provided him with clear, actionable steps to address his challenges, and Coach Bennett's encouragement gave him the confidence to move forward.

"Remember, this is a journey," Coach Bennett said. "You won't get everything right overnight, and that's okay. What matters is that you're taking steps to create the life you want."

James left the office that day with renewed determination. The path ahead would not be easy, but he felt equipped to navigate it for the first time in years. With his coach's support and the strategies they had developed together, James was ready to transform his challenges into opportunities for growth and success.

Chapter 12

Transforming Challenges into Strengths

James Carter's first meeting with Coach Bennett kickstarted a transformative journey. As they worked together, Coach Bennett used cognitive behavioral strategies to tackle the core areas of James' life that were most affected by his ADHD: prioritization and task management, creating structure and routine, enhancing focus and minimizing distractions, managing stress and building resilience, and strengthening communication in his relationships. These strategies helped James regain control and empowered him to turn his challenges into strengths.

Prioritization and Task Management

One of James' most pressing struggles was managing his workload as a project manager. His to-do list was endless, and competing demands often overwhelmed him. Coach Bennett introduced him to the Eisenhower Matrix, a tool that divides tasks into four quadrants based on urgency and importance. Together, they categorized James' tasks:

- **Urgent and Important:** High-priority tasks with immediate deadlines, such as preparing a client presentation.

- **Important but Not Urgent:** Long-term goals like developing a new project proposal.

- **Urgent but Not Important:** Tasks that could be delegated, like scheduling team meetings.

- **Neither Urgent nor Important:** Distractions that could be minimized or eliminated.

James learned to focus on the most impactful tasks while delegating or deferring others using this system. Coach Bennett also helped James implement task chunking, breaking down larger projects into smaller, manageable steps. For example, instead of thinking about completing an entire project, James focused on individual tasks like outlining goals, assigning responsibilities, and scheduling milestones. This approach reduced his feelings of overwhelm and allowed him to make steady progress.

To stay on track, James began using a digital task manager app, where he could set reminders and deadlines for each step. This tool provided both structure and accountability, making it easier for James to manage his responsibilities effectively.

Creating Structure and Routine

A lack of structure had been a major source of stress for James, both at work and at home. Coach Bennett emphasized the importance of establishing routines to create predictability and reduce decision fatigue. They started with James' mornings, designing a simple routine to set the tone for the day:

1. Wake up at 6:30 AM.
2. Spend 15 minutes reviewing his planner and prioritizing tasks.
3. Eat breakfast while skimming the day's emails.
4. Begin work with a clear sense of direction.

Evenings were structured to help James transition from work to relaxation. His wind-down routine included tidying his workspace, reviewing the day's accomplishments, and spending quality time with his wife. These routines provided a sense of stability and allowed James to approach each day intentionally.

Coach Bennett also introduced time-blocking, a cognitive behavioral strategy in which James allocated specific time slots for focused work on individual tasks. For example, he dedicated the first two hours of each morning to high-priority projects and reserved the afternoon for meetings and administrative work. By assigning tasks to specific time blocks, James minimized the mental clutter that often derailed his productivity.

Enhancing Focus and Minimizing Distractions

Staying focused had always been challenging for James, especially during long meetings or when working on tasks that did not interest him immediately. Coach Bennett taught James several strategies to enhance his focus and reduce distractions.

First, they tackled James' tendency to multitask, which often left him feeling scattered and unproductive. James practiced focusing on one task at a time. He turned off email and app notifications during focused work periods to support this shift, using technology boundaries to create a distraction-free environment.

Coach Bennett also recommended the Pomodoro Technique, where James worked in 25-minute intervals followed by 5-minute breaks. This method helped James maintain his focus while giving his brain regular opportunities to recharge. He found it particularly effective for tackling tedious tasks, as the short work intervals made them feel more manageable.

In meetings, James used mindfulness techniques to stay engaged. Before each meeting, he practiced deep breathing to calm his mind and center his attention. During the discussion, he jotted down key points in a notebook to keep his thoughts organized and ensure he contributed meaningfully. These strategies improved James' focus and enhanced his confidence in professional settings.

Managing Stress and Building Resilience

Stress had been a constant companion in James' life, exacerbating his ADHD symptoms and creating a cycle of avoidance and guilt. Coach Bennett introduced several stress management techniques rooted in cognitive behavioral principles to break this cycle.

One strategy was reframing negative thoughts. James often viewed mistakes as personal failures, which fueled his anxiety and self-doubt. Coach Bennett encouraged him to see mistakes as learning opportunities, shifting his mindset from self-criticism to self-compassion. For instance, when James missed a deadline, he focused on identifying what went wrong and how he could improve next time instead of dwelling on his error.

Another key technique was journaling. James spent 10 minutes writing about his accomplishments, challenges, and feelings each evening. This practice helped him process emotions, recognize patterns in his behavior, and celebrate small wins. Over time, journaling became a powerful tool for self-reflection and growth.

Coach Bennett also emphasized the importance of physical activity in managing stress. James began taking short walks during his Pomodoro breaks and started attending a weekly yoga class with his wife. These activities reduced his stress and strengthened his resilience, enabling him to approach challenges with greater clarity and composure.

Strengthening Communication in Relationships

James' ADHD had created tension in his marriage, as his forgetfulness and lack of follow-through often left his wife feeling unsupported. Coach Bennett worked with James to improve communication and strengthen their relationship.

One strategy was proactive communication. James and his wife began scheduling weekly check-ins to discuss household responsibilities, upcoming plans, and any concerns. These conversations created a space for open dialogue and allowed them to address issues before they escalated.

To manage shared responsibilities, they used a digital chore tracker, where they could assign tasks and set reminders. This tool reduced misunderstandings and ensured that both partners were contributing equally to household duties.

James also practiced active listening, a skill that involved giving his wife his full attention during conversations, summarizing her points, and asking clarifying questions. This approach helped James stay present and made his wife feel heard and valued.

Finally, Coach Bennett encouraged James to express gratitude regularly. Whether it was a heartfelt thank you for his wife's support or a small note of appreciation, these gestures strengthened their connection and reminded them of the partnership they were building together.

A Path Forward

Through his work with Coach Bennett, James discovered that cognitive behavioral strategies were more than just tools for managing ADHD; they were a framework for living a more intentional and fulfilling life. By systematically addressing his challenges and building on his strengths, James improved his work performance, deepened his relationships, and regained his confidence.

While the journey was far from over, James felt equipped to face the road ahead. With each strategy he practiced, he took another step toward transforming his challenges into strengths, proving that success was within reach with the right tools and mindset.

Chapter 13

Building Momentum Through Practice

James Carter's journey to implement the strategies he learned from Coach Bennett was one of commitment, growth, and resilience. Over several weeks, he began practicing the cognitive behavioral strategies that addressed his ADHD-related challenges in prioritization, task management, structure, focus, stress management, and relationships. His progress was marked by small victories and a major setback that tested his resolve. Ultimately, his ability to bounce back demonstrated the transformative power of these strategies.

Week 1: Laying the Groundwork

James started by focusing on the basics: prioritization and task management. He spent 15 minutes with his digital task manager each morning, sorting his to-do list into categories using the Eisenhower Matrix. He prioritized tasks in the "Urgent and Important" quadrant and delegated to others whenever possible. By breaking down larger projects into smaller, manageable steps, he began to feel less overwhelmed.

At work, James used the Pomodoro Technique to structure his day. He set a timer for 25-minute work intervals, dedicating each session to a specific task. During his 5-minute breaks, he would stretch, grab water, or jot down any unrelated thoughts that popped into his head. This method helped him stay focused and productive, even when tackling tedious tasks.

James and his wife created a shared chore tracker to divide household responsibilities at home. They sat down together to assign tasks for the week and set reminders for recurring duties. This proactive approach eased tension in their relationship and provided a sense of shared accountability.

Week 2: Strengthening Structure and Routine

In the second week, James concentrated on creating consistent routines. Mornings became smoother as he followed his planned sequence of waking up, reviewing his priorities, eating breakfast, and starting work with a clear direction. Evenings were dedicated to winding down, which included tidying his workspace, reflecting on the day's achievements, and spending time with his wife.

James also integrated mindfulness exercises into his daily routine. Before meetings, he practiced deep breathing to center his attention. During work sessions, he used his notebook to capture stray thoughts, ensuring they did not derail his focus. These practices gave James a sense of control over his day and reduced his anxiety about managing competing demands.

Week 3: Gaining Confidence

By the third week, James was beginning to see tangible improvements. Tasks that once felt insurmountable now seemed manageable. He was meeting deadlines at work, his email inbox was no longer overflowing, and his team noticed a positive change in his focus during meetings.

James and his wife scheduled a weekly check-in at home to discuss household responsibilities, upcoming events, and any concerns. These conversations improved their communication and strengthened their partnership. James also consciously expressed gratitude for his wife's support, which further deepened their connection.

The Setback

Despite his progress, James encountered a significant setback during the fourth week. An unexpected surge of projects at work left him feeling overwhelmed. Faced with tight deadlines, he reverted to old habits of procrastination and multitasking. Tasks piled up, and James missed essential details and fell behind.

The tipping point came when a critical client presentation—one James had been leading—was poorly received. His team's feedback was candid: they felt unprepared and unsupported. James was devastated. He spent the evening replaying the events in his mind, consumed by guilt and frustration. The setback also affected his home life. His wife noticed his stress and withdrawal, which created tension between them.

Bouncing Back

Determined not to let this setback define him, James contacted Coach Bennett for an emergency session. James shared his struggles during their meeting and reflected on what had gone wrong. Coach Bennett acknowledged James' disappointment but reminded him that setbacks were a natural part of growth.

"The key," Coach Bennett said, "is to identify what triggered this lapse and use it as a learning opportunity. You've made tremendous progress, James, and this is just a bump in the road."

Together, they reviewed James' workload and identified the root causes of his struggles. They realized that James had overcommitted to tasks, failing to delegate or set realistic boundaries. This led to a bottleneck of responsibilities that overwhelmed his ability to focus.

Coach Bennett helped James create a recovery plan:

1. **Reprioritize Tasks:** James revisited his to-do list, identifying the most critical items and delegating non-essential tasks to colleagues.
2. **Reset Expectations:** James communicated with his team and supervisor, acknowledging his oversight and setting more realistic timelines for upcoming projects.
3. **Reinforce Routines:** James recommitted to his morning planning sessions and time-blocking schedule to regain structure in his day.

4. **Practice Self-Compassion:** Instead of dwelling on his mistakes, James focused on the lessons he could carry forward.

At home, James opened up to his wife about his struggles and apologized for his recent withdrawal. They scheduled a date night to reconnect, which helped rebuild their emotional bond. James also recommitted to their shared chore tracker, ensuring he stayed accountable for his responsibilities.

Moving Forward

In the weeks following his setback, James found renewed motivation to practice his strategies. He approached his tasks with greater clarity, setting boundaries to prevent overcommitment and regularly checking in with his team to ensure alignment. His focus during meetings improved as he continued using mindfulness and single-tasking techniques.

At home, James' efforts to improve communication and share responsibilities strengthened his relationship with his wife. Their weekly check-ins became a cornerstone of their partnership, fostering trust and collaboration.

By the end of the sixth week, James felt more confident than ever. The setback, while challenging, had taught him valuable lessons about balance, boundaries, and resilience. He realized that progress was not about perfection but about consistently showing up and adapting to challenges.

The Path to Mastery

James' journey was far from over, but he had built a solid foundation for continued growth. The cognitive behavioral strategies he practiced—combined with his determination and support from Coach Bennett—allowed him to navigate setbacks and celebrate successes. Each day was an opportunity to build momentum, turning small victories into lasting change.

This chapter of James' life demonstrated the power of persistence and adaptability. By practicing these strategies and learning from his challenges, James proved that with the right tools and mindset, it was possible to transform struggles into strengths and create a fulfilling life.

Chapter 14

Laura's Story

Laura Kim walked into her office, juggling a stack of reports, her coffee mug, and her phone. It was only 8:00 AM, and she already felt behind. At 41, Laura was a dedicated marketing executive at a large corporation, known for her creative campaigns and ability to connect with clients. Yet, beneath her polished professional exterior, she felt she was barely holding it all together. Her days were a whirlwind of meetings, deadlines, and presentations, leaving little time for her personal life. At home, she faced the additional challenge of being a single mother to her energetic 10-year-old son, Ethan. Balancing the demands of her career and family felt like an impossible task, a reality exacerbated by her recent ADHD diagnosis.

Laura had always known she was different. As a child, her teachers described her as "bright but scattered." She excelled in creative projects but struggled to follow through on more structured assignments. She often misplaced homework, forgot deadlines, and had difficulty staying focused in class. Her parents chalked it up to daydreaming, and Laura learned to compensate by relying on her intelligence and charm to get by.

In her 20s and 30s, Laura's natural charisma and out-of-the-box thinking served her well in advertising. She climbed the corporate ladder quickly, gaining recognition for her innovative ideas and strong client relationships. But as her responsibilities increased, so did the cracks in her coping mechanisms. Laura was overwhelmed by the sheer volume of tasks she managed, and her disorganization began to affect her performance. She missed deadlines, forgot essential meetings, and struggled to keep her team on track.

The Struggles at Work

Laura's ADHD symptoms significantly impacted her professional life. Her desk was perpetually cluttered with papers, sticky notes, and half-empty coffee cups, making it difficult to find what she needed. Emails often went unanswered for days, buried under a flood of new messages. Laura's calendar was often double-booked, leading to frantic rescheduling and strained relationships with colleagues.

During meetings, Laura's mind frequently wandered. She would lose track of the discussion or jump in with ideas that, while creative, were tangential to the topic at hand. Her team appreciated her energy and vision but sometimes grew frustrated with her lack of follow-through. They relied on Laura for direction, but her tendency to procrastinate or focus on less critical tasks left them feeling unsupported.

The pressure to perform at a high level in her role was immense. Laura often worked late into the night to compensate for lost productivity during the day, sacrificing sleep and personal time. Her exhaustion only worsened her ADHD symptoms, creating a vicious cycle that felt impossible to break.

The Challenges at Home

At home, Laura's ADHD affected her ability to be the organized and present parent she wanted to be for Ethan. Mornings were chaotic, with misplaced backpacks, forgotten permission slips, and last-minute scrambles to make it to school on time. Evenings were not much better, as Laura juggled cooking dinner, helping with homework, and preparing for the next day. She often felt guilty about not being more available for her son, worrying that her struggles were affecting his sense of stability.

Ethan, who was beginning to show signs of ADHD himself, required extra support and structure. Laura wanted to be a consistent and reliable presence for him, but her organization and time management difficulties made this challenging. The emotional toll of feeling like she was failing at work and as a parent weighed heavily on her.

The Emotional Impact

Laura's struggles took a significant toll on her mental health. She often felt like she was falling short in every area of her life, no matter how hard she tried. Her confidence, once one of her greatest strengths, was eroding under the weight of self-doubt. She worried that her colleagues and friends would see her as incompetent or unreliable if they knew the extent of her difficulties.

Anxiety became a constant companion, amplifying her ADHD symptoms and making it even harder to focus and stay organized. Laura would lie awake at night, replaying the day's mistakes and worrying about the tasks she had not completed. This cycle of anxiety and overwhelm left her feeling drained and disconnected from the things she once enjoyed.

The Turning Point

Laura's journey toward understanding and addressing her ADHD began when Ethan's teacher suggested he be evaluated for the condition. As she researched ADHD to support her son, Laura started to recognize her symptoms in the descriptions she read. Encouraged by a close friend, she sought out a specialist and was officially diagnosed with ADHD at 40.

While the diagnosis provided clarity, it also came with mixed emotions. Laura felt a sense of relief at finally having an explanation for her struggles. Still, she also grieved the years she had spent trying to compensate without understanding why certain things felt so much harder for her than for others. She wondered how her life might have been different if she had been diagnosed earlier.

Seeking Support

Determined to make a change, Laura began exploring options for managing her ADHD. She read books and articles, joined online support groups, and experimented with different tools and strategies. While these efforts helped, she realized she needed more personalized guidance to address her challenges.

Laura then decided to work with an ADHD coach. She wanted someone to help her create systems that worked for her unique brain and provide accountability as she implemented new habits. Her first session with Coach Julia Wong was a turning point. Julia listened without judgment as Laura described her struggles and goals, reassuring her that change was possible.

The Road Ahead

Laura felt a renewed sense of hope as she embarked on her coaching journey. She knew it would not be easy, but she was ready to invest in herself and her future. Through her sessions with Coach Wong, Laura began to identify the specific areas of her life impacted by ADHD and develop strategies to address them. From building better routines to improving communication with her son and colleagues, she started taking steps toward a more balanced and fulfilling life.

Laura's story is one of resilience and determination. Despite her challenges, she never stopped striving to be the best version of herself. Her journey reminds us that it's never too late to seek help and make meaningful changes. In this chapter, we will delve deeper into Laura's experiences, exploring how she navigated her ADHD diagnosis and the strategies she used to overcome her challenges. Her story offers hope and inspiration to anyone overwhelmed by work, family, and life demands.

Chapter 15

A Blueprint for Balance

Laura Kim's decision to work with an ADHD coach was both a leap of faith and an act of self-care. After years of navigating the chaos of her professional and personal life, she was ready to embrace a structured approach to address her challenges. Her first session with Coach Julia Wong began a journey toward clarity and balance.

Coach Wong had years of experience helping adults with ADHD develop practical strategies to thrive in their careers and personal lives. Her coaching philosophy was rooted in understanding each client's strengths and challenges and creating tailored solutions. Laura arrived at her first session with hope and apprehension, clutching a notebook filled with scattered thoughts about what she wanted to improve.

"Laura, I'm glad you're here," Coach Wong said warmly. "This is a safe space where we'll work together to identify what's holding you back and create systems that support your success. Let's start by talking about what brought you here."

The Assessment

Laura began by describing her struggles in both work and home environments. At work, she felt constantly overwhelmed by the demands of her role as a marketing executive. Her inability to prioritize tasks often left her scrambling to meet deadlines, and her tendency to procrastinate only compounded the problem. Meetings were another challenge; she frequently lost focus or became sidetracked by unrelated ideas. While her creativity was valued, her colleagues sometimes grew frustrated with her lack of organization and follow-through.

At home, Laura's ADHD made it difficult to maintain a sense of order. Mornings with her 10-year-old son, Ethan, were chaotic, with forgotten backpacks and last-minute scrambles to get out the door. Evenings were not much better, as Laura juggled homework help, meal prep, and her unfinished work. She often felt guilty about not being more present for Ethan and worried about the impact of her disorganization on his development.

Coach Wong listened attentively, asking clarifying questions and taking detailed notes. She reassured Laura that her struggles were common among adults with ADHD and that change was entirely possible. "The challenges you've described are valid and important," Coach Wong said. "Now, let's work together to create a plan that addresses these areas systematically."

The assessment involved several key components:

1. **Daily Routines:** Laura described a typical day, highlighting the moments when she felt most productive and struggled.

2. **Strengths and Challenges:** Coach Wong encouraged Laura to identify her strengths, such as her creativity and problem-solving skills, as well as her primary areas of difficulty, including time management and organization.

3. **Stressors and Triggers:** They discussed the factors that heightened Laura's ADHD symptoms, such as tight deadlines, cluttered spaces, and lack of sleep.

4. **Goals and Priorities:** Laura shared her goals for coaching, including improving her work performance, creating a more organized home environment, and spending quality time with Ethan.

By the end of the assessment, Coach Wong clearly understood Laura's needs and was ready to develop a customized coaching plan.

Developing the Coaching Plan

Coach Wong outlined a coaching plan focused on five key areas: prioritization and task management, creating structure and routine, enhancing focus and minimizing distractions, managing stress and building resilience, and improving parenting strategies. Each area was tailored to address Laura's unique challenges while leveraging her strengths.

1. Prioritization and Task Management

Coach Wong introduced Laura to the Eisenhower Matrix, a tool for categorizing tasks based on urgency and importance. Together, they practiced sorting Laura's to-do list into four quadrants:

- **Urgent and Important:** Tasks that required immediate attention, such as preparing for a client presentation.
- **Important but Not Urgent:** Long-term goals, like creating a strategy for an upcoming campaign.
- **Urgent but Not Important:** Tasks that could be delegated, such as scheduling meetings.
- **Neither Urgent nor Important:** Distractions, like non-essential emails.

Laura began using this framework daily to clarify her priorities. Coach Wong also encouraged her to break down larger projects into smaller steps and schedule each step on her calendar. This approach made overwhelming tasks feel more manageable.

2. Creating Structure and Routine

Recognizing that Laura's days lacked structure, Coach Wong helped her design consistent routines for both work and home. Mornings began with a 10-minute planning session, during which Laura reviewed her priorities and set specific goals for the day. Evenings included a wind-down routine that involved tidying her workspace, preparing for the next day, and spending time with Ethan.

Coach Wong suggested using a visual timer to keep Laura on track during focused work periods and a digital planner for scheduling tasks and reminders to support her routines. These tools provided the structure Laura needed to stay organized.

3. Enhancing Focus and Minimizing Distractions

Laura practiced the Pomodoro Technique to improve her focus, working in 25-minute intervals with 5-minute breaks. This method helped her sustain attention while preventing burnout. She used a notebook during meetings to jot down key points and action items, ensuring she stayed engaged and retained important information.

Coach Wong also helped Laura identify her primary distractions, such as notifications and clutter. Together, they developed strategies to address these issues, including silencing her phone during work sessions and creating a designated space for important documents.

4. Managing Stress and Building Resilience

Stress management was a critical component of Laura's plan. Coach Wong encouraged her to incorporate mindfulness practices, such as deep breathing exercises and short meditation breaks, into her daily routine. These practices helped Laura stay calm and centered, even during high-pressure situations.

To build resilience, Laura began journaling each evening to reflect on her accomplishments and challenges. This practice allowed her to recognize her progress and identify patterns in her behavior. Coach Wong also encouraged Laura to prioritize self-care, such as getting enough sleep and engaging in activities she enjoyed, like yoga and painting.

5. Improving Parenting Strategies

As a single mother, Laura wanted to create a more supportive and structured environment for Ethan. Coach Wong suggested establishing clear morning and evening routines, such as setting out clothes and packing lunches the night before. They also discussed strategies for helping Ethan with his homework, including breaking tasks into smaller steps and using positive reinforcement to celebrate his efforts.

Coach Wong emphasized the importance of open communication between Laura and Ethan. Together, they brainstormed ways to involve Ethan in household responsibilities, fostering a sense of teamwork and mutual support.

Moving Forward

Laura felt a renewed sense of purpose and hope as the session ended. Coach Wong provided her with a list of action items to work on before their next meeting, reminding her to be patient with herself as she implemented these changes. "Progress takes time," Coach Wong said. "Remember to celebrate small wins and credit yourself for every step you take."

Laura left the session with a clear plan and the tools to make meaningful changes. For the first time in years, she felt like she had a roadmap to navigate the complexities of her life. The journey ahead would not be without challenges, but Laura was ready to embrace the process and build a life of balance and fulfillment.

Chapter 16
Strategies for a Balanced Life

Laura Kim's first session with Coach Julia Wong was the beginning of a transformative journey. Through cognitive behavioral strategies, Coach Wong helped Laura address the core areas of her life impacted by ADHD: prioritization and task management, creating structure and routine, enhancing focus and minimizing distractions, managing stress and building resilience, and improving parenting strategies. Together, they created actionable solutions to turn Laura's challenges into strengths.

Prioritization and Task Management

One of Laura's most pressing challenges was the overwhelming number of tasks she needed to juggle daily. At work, she struggled to identify what required her immediate attention, often bouncing between projects and losing sight of deadlines. Coach Wong introduced her to the Eisenhower Matrix, a cognitive tool that categorizes tasks based on their urgency and importance.

Together, they sorted Laura's responsibilities into four quadrants:

- **Urgent and Important:** Tasks requiring immediate attention, like preparing for a client presentation.

- **Important but Not Urgent:** Long-term projects, such as strategy planning for an upcoming campaign.

- **Urgent but Not Important:** Tasks that could be delegated, like scheduling team meetings.

- **Neither Urgent nor Important:** Distractions, such as excessive email notifications.

This exercise provided Laura with clarity on where to focus her energy. Coach Wong encouraged her to use a digital task manager app to support her prioritization further. Laura began breaking large projects into smaller, manageable tasks, assigning deadlines for each step. This reduced her overwhelm and allowed her to track her progress and celebrate small victories.

Creating Structure and Routine

Laura's lack of consistent routines often left her feeling ungrounded and frazzled. Mornings with her son, Ethan, were especially chaotic as they scrambled to get out the door on time. Coach Wong emphasized the importance of establishing predictable routines to create stability and reduce decision fatigue.

They started by designing a structured morning schedule for Laura and Ethan. The routine included:

1. Waking up at 6:30 AM.
2. Preparing breakfast and reviewing the day's plans with Ethan.
3. Packing lunches and setting out clothes the night before to streamline the morning process.

Evenings were similarly structured, with time dedicated to tidying up, preparing for the next day, and engaging in a relaxing activity before bed. Coach Wong introduced Laura to habit stacking, a cognitive strategy for pairing new habits with existing ones. For example, Laura began reviewing her digital planner while sipping her morning coffee, integrating productivity into a familiar routine.

Enhancing Focus and Minimizing Distractions

Focus was another area where Laura struggled, especially during long meetings or when working on tasks that did not immediately engage her. Coach Wong helped Laura implement strategies to enhance her attention and minimize distractions.

The Pomodoro Technique became one of Laura's go-to tools. Working in 25-minute intervals followed by 5-minute breaks made it easier to maintain focus and manage her energy. During these breaks, she stretched, took short walks, or enjoyed a moment of mindfulness to recharge.

To tackle distractions, Laura created a designated workspace free from clutter and distractions. She silenced notifications on her phone and email during work sessions, using a notebook to jot down unrelated thoughts or ideas for later. This "thought parking lot" approach allowed her to stay on task without losing track of important insights.

During meetings, Laura practiced active listening, taking concise notes to retain key points, and staying present by summarizing the discussion in her own words. These strategies improved her participation and confidence, earning her positive colleague feedback.

Managing Stress and Building Resilience

The constant demands of work and parenting often left Laura feeling overwhelmed and anxious. Coach Wong helped her develop stress management techniques rooted in cognitive behavioral principles.

One key strategy was reframing negative thoughts. Laura often felt like she was failing as a professional and a parent, but Coach Wong encouraged her to challenge these beliefs by focusing on her successes. For instance, when Laura completed a significant work project, she took time to acknowledge her effort and competence rather than dwelling on minor setbacks.

Mindfulness exercises became a cornerstone of Laura's stress management routine. During her breaks, she practiced deep breathing and guided meditation, which helped her stay grounded and reduce anxiety.

Journaling also provided an outlet for processing her emotions and identifying patterns in her thoughts and behaviors.

To build resilience, Laura incorporated self-care into her routine. She began attending a weekly yoga class, which became a cherished time for relaxation and reflection. She also prioritized getting enough sleep, recognizing its critical role in managing her ADHD symptoms.

Improving Parenting Strategies

As a single mother, Laura wanted to create a supportive and structured environment for Ethan. Coach Wong worked with her to develop parenting strategies that fostered teamwork and mutual understanding.

They started by establishing clear routines for Ethan, mirroring the structure Laura was building in her own life. Together, they created a morning checklist for Ethan, including tasks like brushing his teeth, packing his backpack, and reviewing his homework. Visual cues, such as colorful charts and sticky notes, made the routine engaging and easy for Ethan to follow.

Homework time was another area of focus. Coach Wong suggested breaking assignments into smaller steps and setting a timer for focused work sessions, similar to the Pomodoro Technique Laura used. Positive reinforcement, like praise or small rewards, motivated Ethan to stay on track and complete his tasks.

Open communication became a priority in their relationship. Laura scheduled regular check-ins with Ethan to discuss his feelings, challenges, and achievements. These conversations strengthened their bond and gave Laura insight into how she could better support him.

Coach Wong also encouraged Laura to involve Ethan in household responsibilities. Laura fostered a sense of independence and teamwork by assigning age-appropriate tasks, such as setting the table or organizing his toys. This approach lightened Laura's load and empowered Ethan to contribute to their shared environment.

The Impact of Cognitive Behavioral Strategies

As Laura implemented these strategies, she began to see profound changes in her daily life. Her ability to prioritize tasks and maintain a structured routine allowed her to approach each day more confidently and clearly. The techniques she used to enhance focus and minimize distractions improved her productivity and reduced her feelings of overwhelm.

The structured routines and parenting strategies at home created a more harmonious environment for Laura and Ethan. Their mornings became smoother, their evenings more connected, and their relationship stronger than ever. Laura no longer felt like she was constantly falling short; instead, she celebrated her and Ethan's progress together.

Through stress management and resilience-building practices, Laura learned to navigate challenges with greater ease. She recognized the value of self-compassion and embraced the idea that growth was a journey, not a destination. By focusing on her strengths and systematically addressing her challenges, Laura began to build a life of balance and fulfillment.

Coach Wong's guidance and the cognitive-behavioral strategies they practiced together transformed Laura's approach to her ADHD and her life. Her story is a testament to the power of persistence and the potential for meaningful change, offering hope and inspiration to anyone facing similar struggles.

Chapter 17

Building Resilience Through Practice

Laura Kim's journey to implement the strategies she learned with Coach Wong was filled with small victories, moments of self-doubt, and profound growth. Over several weeks, Laura practiced prioritization, structure, focus, stress management, and improved parenting strategies. Despite a significant setback, she demonstrated the resilience to adapt and move forward.

Week 1: Taking the First Steps

Laura began by integrating prioritization and task management strategies into her workday. She started each morning with a 10-minute planning session, using the Eisenhower Matrix to sort her tasks into categories. This helped her focus on high-priority projects while delegating less critical tasks to her team. Breaking down large projects into smaller, manageable steps made her workload feel more achievable.

At home, Laura introduced a morning checklist for her son, Ethan, to streamline their chaotic mornings. The checklist included simple tasks like brushing his teeth, packing his backpack, and reviewing his homework. By setting out clothes and preparing lunches the night before, Laura and Ethan both started their days with less stress.

In the evenings, Laura committed to her new wind-down routine, which included tidying her workspace, reflecting on the day's accomplishments, and preparing for the next day. These practices gave her a sense of control and helped her approach each day with clarity.

Week 2: Gaining Momentum

In the second week, Laura focused on enhancing her focus and minimizing distractions. She adopted the Pomodoro Technique, setting a timer for 25-minute work intervals followed by 5-minute breaks. This approach kept her energy levels consistent and made long tasks feel less daunting. To recharge, she practiced mindfulness exercises during her breaks, such as deep breathing and stretching.

Laura also tackled her cluttered workspace, dedicating an afternoon to decluttering and organizing her office. She created designated spaces for important documents and supplies, making it easier to find what she needed. She silenced notifications on her phone and email during focused work sessions to reduce distractions.

At home, Laura encouraged Ethan to take responsibility for small household tasks, such as setting the table or organizing his toys. This lightened Laura's load and fostered a sense of teamwork and independence in Ethan.

Week 3: Building Confidence

By the third week, Laura began to see tangible improvements. Her ability to prioritize tasks and stay focused during meetings earned her praise from colleagues, and her new routines at home made mornings and evenings smoother. Ethan responded well to the structure, showing more independence and cooperation.

Laura also found herself managing stress more effectively. Journaling each evening helped her process emotions and recognize her progress, while yoga and mindfulness exercises provided a sense of calm amidst her busy schedule. These practices gave her the resilience to handle unexpected challenges without feeling overwhelmed.

The Setback

Despite her progress, Laura faced a significant setback in the fourth week. A last-minute request from a high-profile client disrupted her carefully planned schedule. Feeling pressured to deliver, Laura worked late into the night, neglecting her evening routine and skipping her usual self-care practices. The following morning, she woke up exhausted and rushed, which threw off her entire day.

At work, Laura's exhaustion made it difficult for her to focus during meetings, and she struggled to keep up with her tasks. At home, the lack of structure spilled over into her interactions with Ethan, leading to a tense evening in which both felt frustrated. The setback left Laura questioning whether she could sustain the changes she had worked so hard to implement.

Bouncing Back

Determined not to let the setback derail her progress, Laura reached out to Coach Wong for guidance. During their session, they reviewed what had happened and identified the triggers that led to the lapse. Coach Wong reminded Laura that setbacks were a natural part of the growth process and an opportunity to learn and adapt.

Together, they developed a plan to address the situation:

1. **Reevaluate Priorities:** Laura revisited her to-do list, identifying tasks that could be deferred or delegated to free up time for the client's request without sacrificing her routines.

2. **Strengthen Boundaries:** Laura practiced setting realistic expectations with her clients and colleagues, ensuring she had the bandwidth to manage unexpected demands without overwhelming herself.

3. **Recommit to Self-Care:** Laura returned to her wind-down routine and made self-care non-negotiable, recognizing its importance in maintaining her energy and focus.

Laura also spoke openly with Ethan about the challenges they faced that week. She acknowledged her own mistakes and emphasized the importance of working together as a team. This transparency strengthened their bond and reinforced the value of communication.

Moving Forward

In the weeks that followed, Laura approached her strategies with renewed determination. She continued practicing prioritization, task management, and focus techniques while being mindful of her limits and setting boundaries when needed. Her routines became a cornerstone of her success, providing stability and clarity amidst her busy life.

At home, Laura and Ethan maintained their morning and evening routines, which created a sense of predictability and teamwork. Their relationship grew stronger as they worked together to navigate challenges and celebrate progress.

Laura's ability to bounce back from her setback demonstrated her resilience and commitment to growth. She realized that success was not about avoiding mistakes but about learning from them and continuing to move forward. By embracing this mindset, Laura built a foundation for lasting change and a more balanced, fulfilling life.

The Path Ahead

Laura's journey was a testament to the power of persistence and the effectiveness of cognitive behavioral strategies. Her practice and resilience transformed her challenges into opportunities for growth. The skills she developed improved her work performance and parenting and deepened her confidence and self-compassion.

As she continued her journey, Laura felt more equipped to face the complexities of her life with clarity and purpose. Her story is an inspiring example of what's possible when we embrace change, adapt to setbacks, and stay committed to our goals.

Chapter 18
Nathan's Story

Nathan Reed's desk was a monument to his brilliance and chaos. Scattered across its surface were scribbled notes, open coding manuals, energy drink cans, and a well-worn laptop adorned with stickers of his favorite programming languages. At 27, Nathan was already making a name for himself as a software engineer at a cutting-edge tech startup. His ability to tackle complex problems and deliver innovative solutions set him apart in an industry filled with talented minds. Yet, behind his professional success lay a hidden struggle that shaped both his achievements and his challenges: ADHD.

Growing up, Nathan's parents quickly realized he was different. While other children would lose interest in toys after a few days, Nathan would spend weeks meticulously building and rebuilding elaborate LEGO creations. His teachers noted his incredible aptitude for math and science but often lamented his disorganization and inability to stay on task during routine assignments. Diagnosed with ADHD in middle school, Nathan's hyperfocus on subjects he loved and his neglect of everything else became a defining feature of his life.

Early Years: A Curious Mind

As a child, Nathan's curiosity knew no bounds. He was the kind of kid who dismantled his family's toaster to see how it worked. While his parents admired his curiosity, they grew frustrated with his inability to complete basic chores or homework. In school, Nathan excelled in subjects he found engaging, like computer science and physics, but barely scraped by in others, such as history and English. His teachers often described him as "brilliant but distracted."

Nathan's ADHD diagnosis provided some clarity, but his family struggled to find strategies that could help him. Traditional methods like rigid schedules and study plans often backfired, leaving Nathan feeling constrained and unmotivated. Instead, he developed coping mechanisms, relying on his natural intelligence and charm to navigate challenges. While this approach got him through high school, it set the stage for his struggles as an adult.

The College Years: Freedom and Focus

College was both liberating and overwhelming for Nathan. Freed from the rigid structure of high school, he thrived in the areas he was passionate about, spending countless hours in the computer lab writing code and developing apps. His professors praised his innovative thinking and willingness to tackle complex problems, often citing him as one of the brightest students they had ever taught.

However, the freedom of college also exacerbated Nathan's struggles with time management and organization. He frequently missed deadlines for assignments in non-technical courses, prioritizing his coding projects over everything else. Late nights in the lab became the norm, leaving him sleep-deprived and struggling to keep up with the demands of his coursework. Despite these challenges, Nathan graduated with honors, earning a degree in computer science and landing a coveted job at a tech startup.

Professional Life: Brilliance and Burnout

Nathan's career as a software engineer was a natural fit for his skills and interests. His ability to dive deeply into problems and uncover innovative solutions quickly earned him a reputation as one of the most talented engineers at his company. Nathan thrived on the creative aspects of his work, mainly designing algorithms and developing new features for the company's flagship products. His colleagues marveled at his ability to produce high-quality work under pressure, often joking that Nathan's brain was a supercomputer.

However, Nathan's ADHD also created significant challenges in his professional life. While he excelled at tasks he enjoyed, he struggled to stay engaged with less stimulating responsibilities, such as documenting his code, responding to emails, or attending team meetings. These lapses often frustrated his colleagues, who relied on him to provide updates and ensure projects stayed on track.

Nathan's tendency to hyperfocus on enjoyable tasks also led to issues with work-life balance. He frequently lost track of time while coding, working late into the night and neglecting basic needs like eating and sleeping. Over time, this pattern of overworking began to take a toll on his physical and mental health. He became increasingly isolated, as his intense focus on work left little room for maintaining personal relationships.

Emotional Impact

The emotional toll of Nathan's ADHD was significant. While he took pride in his accomplishments, he often felt like he constantly fell short in areas that mattered just as much, if not more. His colleagues' frustration with his missed deadlines and lack of follow-through left him feeling inadequate despite his undeniable brilliance. Nathan frequently doubted his ability to succeed in the long term, worrying that his ADHD would eventually derail his career.

Socially, Nathan struggled to maintain connections with friends and family. His tendency to hyperfocus on work made him unavailable for social gatherings and personal conversations, creating distance between him and his loved ones. While Nathan wanted to be more present, he found it difficult to shift his focus away from his work.

Seeking Help

Nathan's turning point came after a particularly challenging project at work. While his technical contributions were celebrated, his failure to provide clear documentation and respond to his team's requests created significant delays. During a performance review, his manager praised his brilliance but gently pointed out the areas where he needed to improve. For Nathan, this feedback was a wake-up call. He realized that while his ADHD was a source of strength in some areas, it was also holding him back in others.

Encouraged by his manager and a close friend, Nathan began exploring resources to help manage his ADHD. He read books and articles, joined online forums, and experimented with various productivity tools. However, he found it challenging to apply these strategies consistently. Frustrated but determined, Nathan decided to seek professional help and began working with an ADHD coach.

A New Chapter

Nathan's decision to work with a coach began a new chapter in his life. During their initial sessions, his coach helped him identify the specific areas where ADHD was impacting his life and develop tailored strategies to address these challenges. Together, they worked on improving his time management skills, creating systems to ensure he followed through on less enjoyable tasks, and finding ways to balance his work with his personal life.

Before long, Nathan began to see ADHD not just as a challenge but as a part of who he was—a source of both strength and struggle. With the right tools and support, he realized he could harness his unique abilities while addressing the obstacles that had held him back. Nathan's journey is a testament to the power of resilience and the importance of seeking help when needed.

In this chapter, we will delve deeper into Nathan's experiences, exploring his strategies to manage his ADHD and the lessons he learned along the way. His story offers hope and inspiration to anyone navigating the complexities of ADHD, proving determination and support can turn challenges into growth opportunities.

Chapter 19

A Roadmap to Balance and Wellness

Nathan Reed sat nervously across from his ADHD coach, Rebecca Meyers, in her bright and organized office. It was his first session, and while he was eager to find solutions to his struggles, he was not sure what to expect. Rebecca greeted him warmly, her calm demeanor immediately putting him at ease.

"Nathan, I'm so glad you're here," she said. "ADHD can present unique challenges, but it also comes with strengths that we can build on. Today, we're going to assess where you're at and create a plan to help you thrive both personally and professionally."

Nathan came to Rebecca seeking help managing his time, staying accountable to less engaging tasks, and improving his work-life balance. He also admitted, almost as an afterthought, that he often neglected his diet, relying on takeout and snacks to get through his long coding sessions. Rebecca's holistic approach to coaching included addressing these foundational needs, and she was determined to help Nathan create a sustainable roadmap for success.

The Assessment

Rebecca began by asking Nathan to describe his current challenges and daily routines. Nathan noted his tendency to hyperfocus on work he loved, like coding and problem-solving, while neglecting tasks like writing documentation, responding to emails, or attending meetings. He also described his disorganized workspace, overflowing email inbox, and the hours he often spent lost in his projects, neglecting meals, sleep, and social interactions.

"It sounds like your hyperfocus is both a strength and a challenge," Rebecca noted. "It allows you to excel at your work, but it also pulls you away from other responsibilities and self-care. Let's figure out how we can channel that focus more effectively."

Rebecca also explored Nathan's relationship with food and nutrition. Nathan admitted he often forgot to eat or relied on quick, unhealthy options like instant noodles or takeout. "It's not that I don't want to eat well," he explained. "I just get so caught up in work that cooking feels impossible."

Through this comprehensive assessment, Rebecca identified key areas where Nathan needed support:

1. **Time Management and Prioritization:** Balancing engaging tasks with less enjoyable but essential responsibilities.

2. **Organization:** Creating systems to manage his workspace, emails, and workflow.

3. **Work-Life Balance:** Setting boundaries to protect his time for personal relationships and self-care.

4. **Nutrition and Wellness:** Developing simple healthy diet strategies.

Developing the Coaching Plan

With a clear understanding of Nathan's challenges, Rebecca outlined a coaching plan tailored to his needs. "This plan is a starting point," she explained. "We'll adjust it based on what works for you and what doesn't. The goal is to create systems that fit your life and support your success."

1. Time Management and Prioritization

Rebecca introduced Nathan to the Eisenhower Matrix as a tool to prioritize his tasks based on urgency and importance. Together, they practiced sorting Nathan's responsibilities into four categories:

- **Urgent and Important:** Tasks like preparing for a client presentation.

- **Important but Not Urgent:** Long-term goals include developing a new coding feature.

- **Urgent but Not Important:** Tasks that could be delegated, such as scheduling meetings.

- **Neither Urgent nor Important:** Distractions like excessive social media scrolling.

Rebecca also recommended breaking large tasks into smaller, manageable steps. For example, instead of thinking about completing an entire coding project, Nathan could focus on individual milestones like writing the initial code, testing modules, and integrating features. Assigning deadlines to each step helped Nathan stay accountable without feeling overwhelmed.

2. Organization

Rebecca suggested a complete overhaul of his workspace to address Nathan's disorganization. They created a plan for decluttering his desk and setting up systems for his physical and digital materials. Key strategies included:

- **Categorizing Documents:** Using labeled folders for different projects.

- **Creating a Digital Filing System:** Organizing his computer files into clearly named directories.

- **Daily Reset:** Spending five minutes at the end of each day tidying his workspace and reviewing his tasks.

Rebecca also introduced Nathan to a project management tool to track his tasks and deadlines. By centralizing his responsibilities in one place, Nathan could reduce the mental load of remembering everything.

3. Work-Life Balance

Recognizing Nathan's tendency to overwork, Rebecca emphasized the importance of setting boundaries. They worked together to establish "work hours," after which Nathan would step away from his laptop and focus on personal time. She encouraged him to schedule social activities with friends and family to ensure he stayed connected to his support network.

To protect his time for relaxation and hobbies, Nathan began experimenting with time-blocking. He dedicated specific hours to work, meals, exercise, and leisure activities, treating each block as an important appointment.

4. Nutrition and Wellness

Given Nathan's poor eating habits, Rebecca incorporated a nutrition plan into his coaching plan. The focus was on simplicity and sustainability:

- **Meal Prepping:** Rebecca helped Nathan develop a weekly routine for preparing easy, healthy meals in advance, such as grilled chicken, and roasted vegetables.

- **Stocking Healthy Snacks:** Nathan kept items like nuts, yogurt, and fresh fruit on hand for quick energy boosts during work sessions.

- **Setting Reminders to Eat:** Using his phone, Nathan set alarms to remind him to take breaks for meals.

Rebecca also encouraged Nathan to keep a water bottle at his desk and make hydration a priority. "Your brain works better when your body is fueled and hydrated," she explained. "This isn't just about eating; it's about supporting your overall performance and well-being."

The Path Forward

As their session concluded, Rebecca provided Nathan with a list of action items to work on before their next meeting:

1. Start each day with a 10-minute planning session using the Eisenhower Matrix.
2. Dedicate one afternoon to decluttering his workspace and setting up organizational systems.
3. Block off time for meals and leisure activities in his calendar.
4. Experiment with meal prepping over the weekend and stock up on healthy snacks.
5. Reflect on his progress in a journal to identify what's working and what needs adjustment.

"Remember, this is a process," Rebecca said. "We're not aiming for perfection—we're aiming for progress. Every small step you take brings you closer to the balance you're looking for."

Nathan left the session feeling both relieved and motivated. For the first time, he had a clear roadmap to address his ADHD challenges and create a life that supported his strengths while managing his weaknesses. Including a nutrition plan felt like an unexpected but crucial addition, reminding him that success was not just about productivity—it was also about wellness.

Over the coming weeks, Nathan would begin implementing these strategies, building habits that allowed him to thrive in all aspects of his life. His journey was just beginning, but with Rebecca's guidance, he felt ready to take the first steps toward a balanced and fulfilling future.

Chapter 20
Strategies for Sustainable Success

Nathan Reed's first meeting with Coach Rebecca Meyers marked a pivotal moment in his journey to manage ADHD. Through cognitive behavioral strategies, Rebecca helped Nathan address challenges in time management and prioritization, organization, work-life balance, and nutrition and wellness. These strategies not only targeted his ADHD symptoms but also provided a framework for long-term success.

Management and Prioritization

Nathan's hyperfocus on tasks he enjoyed often left other responsibilities neglected. Rebecca introduced him to the Eisenhower Matrix, a tool for categorizing tasks based on urgency and importance. Together, they sorted his responsibilities into four quadrants:

1. **Urgent and Important:** Tasks requiring immediate attention, such as fixing critical bugs in the company's software.

2. **Important but Not Urgent:** Long-term goals, like developing new coding skills.

3. **Urgent but Not Important:** Administrative tasks, such as scheduling meetings, that could be delegated.

4. **Neither Urgent nor Important:** Distractions, like excessive time spent browsing social media.

This exercise gave Nathan a clear picture of where to focus his energy. Rebecca also introduced the concept of task chunking, breaking down large projects into smaller, manageable steps. For instance, instead of viewing a coding project as a single task, Nathan learned to break it into milestones such as writing initial code, testing, and debugging. Assigning deadlines to each step ensured steady progress without feeling overwhelmed.

Nathan practiced starting his day with a 10-minute planning session to prioritize his tasks using the matrix and set achievable goals. This habit gave him a sense of direction and minimized the procrastination that often stemmed from feeling overwhelmed.

Organization

Nathan's workspace and digital files were a source of stress, with clutter making it difficult to find what he needed. Rebecca emphasized the importance of creating systems to organize both physical and digital environments.

They developed a decluttering strategy for his physical workspace. Nathan began by categorizing items into "frequently used," "seldom used," and "unnecessary." He kept frequently used tools within arm's reach, stored seldom-used items in labeled containers, and discarded unnecessary clutter. To maintain this order, Rebecca suggested a daily reset, where Nathan spent five minutes tidying his desk and organizing materials at the end of each workday.

Rebecca guided Nathan in creating a logical folder structure for his digital files. Each project had its own folder, with subfolders for tasks like "Code," "Testing," and "Documentation." File names were standardized to include dates and project details for easy retrieval. A cloud-based system ensured his files were accessible and backed up.

Rebecca also introduced a task management tool to track Nathan's projects and deadlines. Centralizing responsibilities in one platform reduced Nathan's mental load of remembering everything, freeing his mind to focus on his work.

Work-Life Balance

One of Nathan's biggest challenges was his tendency to overwork. He often lost track of time while coding late into the night. Rebecca emphasized the importance of setting boundaries to protect his personal time and relationships.

They established a structured schedule that included designated work hours with clear start and end times. To ensure he adhered to this schedule, Nathan set alarms on his phone as reminders to step away from his desk. Rebecca also encouraged him to schedule non-work activities, such as spending time with friends, exercising, or pursuing hobbies, to create a more balanced routine.

Rebecca introduced time-blocking, a strategy where Nathan allocated specific periods for focused work, meals, and leisure activities. For example, he reserved mornings for deep work on coding projects, afternoons for meetings and administrative tasks, and evenings for relaxation and socializing. Treating these blocks as non-negotiable appointments helped Nathan maintain balance while staying productive.

To strengthen his relationships, Nathan scheduled regular check-ins with friends and family. These intentional efforts to reconnect fostered a sense of support and helped him step away from work more frequently.

Nutrition and Wellness

Nathan's poor eating habits noticeably impacted his energy levels and overall health. Recognizing the importance of nutrition, Rebecca worked with him to create a sustainable plan that fit his busy lifestyle.

They began by identifying simple, healthy meals Nathan could prepare in advance. He started meal prepping on Sundays, making dishes like grilled chicken and roasted vegetables that could be easily reheated during the week. Rebecca also suggested keeping healthy snacks, such as nuts, sugar-free yogurt, and fresh fruit, at his desk to curb hunger during long work sessions.

To address Nathan's tendency to skip meals, Rebecca helped him set reminders on his phone to take breaks for breakfast, lunch, and dinner. These scheduled breaks ensured he ate regularly and allowed him to step away from work and recharge.

Hydration was another focus. Nathan kept a water bottle at his desk and made it a goal to drink a certain amount of water each day. Rebecca explained how proper hydration supported cognitive function and overall well-being, making it essential to his success.

Finally, Rebecca encouraged Nathan to incorporate physical activity into his routine. Whether it was a short walk during a Pomodoro break or a weekly workout session, exercise became a way for Nathan to manage stress and boost his energy levels.

The Impact of Cognitive Behavioral Strategies

As Nathan implemented these strategies, he saw significant changes in his life. Prioritization and task management tools helped him stay on top of responsibilities without feeling overwhelmed. Organizational systems made his workspace and digital files more efficient, reducing stress and saving time. By setting boundaries and practicing time-blocking, Nathan achieved a better work-life balance, strengthening his relationships and improving his overall well-being.

The nutrition plan was a particularly transformative aspect of his journey. Regular meals and healthy snacks gave Nathan the sustained energy he needed to stay productive throughout the day. Meal prepping and hydration habits became cornerstones of his routine, supporting both his physical health and cognitive performance.

Through these cognitive behavioral strategies, Nathan discovered that managing ADHD wasn't about changing who he was but about creating systems that worked with his brain. By addressing his challenges holistically and building on his strengths, he improved his professional performance and created a more fulfilling personal life.

Rebecca's coaching provided Nathan with the tools and confidence to navigate his ADHD with greater clarity and purpose. His journey serves as a reminder that the right strategies and support can turn challenges into opportunities and build a life of balance and success.

Chapter 21

The Road to Mastery

Nathan Reed's journey to implement the strategies he developed with Coach Rebecca Meyers was filled with triumphs and challenges. Over several weeks, he practiced prioritization, organization, work-life balance, and nutrition strategies that transformed his daily life. Yet, his path was not without setbacks, and one particularly challenging week tested his resolve. By applying the tools he learned, Nathan demonstrated resilience and emerged stronger.

Week 1: Starting Small

Nathan began his journey by focusing on the basics. His first goal was to establish a consistent morning planning routine. Each day, he spent 10 minutes using the Eisenhower Matrix to categorize his tasks. By sorting his responsibilities into "Urgent and Important," "Important but Not Urgent," "Urgent but Not Important," and "Neither Urgent nor Important," Nathan gained clarity about where to direct his energy.

He also started task chunking, breaking his coding projects into manageable steps. For example, he divided the work into brainstorming, coding, debugging, and testing phases instead of tackling an entire feature update. This approach made overwhelming tasks feel more achievable.

At home, Nathan tackled his cluttered workspace. He spent an afternoon organizing his desk, setting up labeled folders for physical documents, and restructuring his digital files into a logical hierarchy. By the end of the week, his workspace felt less chaotic, and he found it easier to locate what he needed.

Week 2: Building Momentum

With his routines in place, Nathan expanded his focus to include work-life balance and nutrition. He began using time-blocking to allocate specific periods for work, meals, and leisure activities. Mornings were reserved for deep work on coding projects, afternoons for meetings, and evenings for relaxation or socializing. By treating these blocks as non-negotiable, Nathan ensured he had time for self-care and relationships.

To improve his diet, Nathan started meal prepping on Sundays. He cooked simple dishes like grilled chicken and roasted vegetables, which he portioned into containers for the week. This eliminated the stress of deciding what to eat daily and helped him maintain steady energy levels.

Nathan also kept healthy snacks, such as nuts and fruit, at his desk to curb hunger during work sessions. He set reminders on his phone to drink water and take meal breaks, ensuring he stayed hydrated and nourished.

Week 3: Gaining Confidence

By the third week, Nathan began to see tangible improvements. His morning planning sessions helped him stay organized and on top of his tasks. Colleagues noticed his improved focus and reliability, particularly in meetings where he actively participated and followed through on action items.

Nathan's structured schedule gave him time to reconnect with friends and family. He scheduled regular coffee dates and phone calls, strengthening his relationships and providing a much-needed break from work.

Thanks to his improved diet and hydration habits, Nathan felt more energized physically. Meal prepping and scheduled breaks became second nature, supporting his productivity and overall well-being.

The Setback

Despite his progress, Nathan faced a significant setback during the fourth week. A high-stakes project at work required immediate attention, disrupting his carefully planned schedule. Nathan's hyperfocus kicked in, and he spent hours coding without taking breaks, skipping meals, and neglecting his evening routine. By the end of the week, he was physically and mentally exhausted.

The impact of the setback extended beyond work. Nathan's friends noticed his absence and a missed dinner plan with a close friend caused tension in their relationship. Nathan's progress in work-life balance and nutrition seemed to unravel, leaving him frustrated and doubting his ability to sustain the changes he had made.

Bouncing Back

Determined not to let the setback define him, Nathan scheduled an emergency session with Coach Rebecca. Together, they reviewed what had gone wrong and identified strategies to prevent a similar situation in the future. Rebecca reminded Nathan that setbacks were a natural part of growth and an opportunity to learn.

They devised a plan to help Nathan regain his footing:

1. **Reevaluate Priorities:** Nathan revisited his to-do list, using the Eisenhower Matrix to distinguish between truly urgent tasks and those that could wait. This helped him focus on critical responsibilities without overcommitting.

2. **Reinforce Breaks:** Nathan set alarms on his phone to remind him to take short breaks and eat meals, even during high-pressure situations.

3. **Set Boundaries:** Nathan practiced communicating his limits to his team, ensuring they understood when he needed recharge. He also delegated tasks where possible to lighten his workload.

4. **Recommit to Self-Care:** Nathan returned to his evening routine and meal prep habits, recognizing that self-care was essential to sustaining his performance.

At home, Nathan apologized to his friend and made amends by rescheduling their dinner. This experience reinforced the importance of prioritizing relationships, even during busy periods.

Week 5: Moving Forward

With Rebecca's guidance, Nathan bounced back stronger than before. He approached his routines with renewed commitment and learned to adapt his strategies to fit dynamic situations. By balancing his high-pressure work environment with consistent self-care practices, Nathan discovered a sustainable rhythm.

He continued using time-blocking to protect his personal time and strengthened his boundaries at work. By setting realistic expectations with his team, Nathan ensured he could meet deadlines without sacrificing his well-being.

Nathan's nutrition plan became a cornerstone of his routine. Meal prepping, scheduled breaks, and hydration habits supported his energy and focus, helping him perform at his best.

The Path Ahead

Nathan's journey was a testament to resilience and the effectiveness of cognitive behavioral strategies. While setbacks were inevitable, his ability to learn and adapt made him stronger with each challenge. By practicing these strategies consistently, Nathan transformed his approach to work, relationships, and self-care.

The lessons he learned improved his professional performance and enriched his personal life. Nathan's story reminds us that growth is a process, and even small steps can lead to profound change.

Chapter 22

Lessons from the ADHD Stories

The stories of Sophia Martinez, James Carter, Laura Kim, and Nathan Reed have taken us on a journey through the unique experiences of individuals living with ADHD. Each narrative revealed different challenges, strengths, and transformative moments, providing invaluable insights into the realities of managing ADHD in diverse contexts. By reflecting on their journeys, readers can better understand the nuances of ADHD and the strategies that lead to meaningful change.

Sophia's Story: The Determined College Student

Sophia's story illustrates the trials of balancing academic responsibilities while managing ADHD. As a college student, her struggles with procrastination, poor time management, and a sense of overwhelm mirrored the experiences of many young adults navigating ADHD. Through coaching, Sophia learned the importance of structure, daily routines, and prioritization. Strategies such as time-blocking, the Pomodoro Technique, and breaking tasks into manageable steps helped her regain control and confidence in her academic life.

Sophia teaches us the value of consistency and starting small. Her transformation demonstrated that building habits, even incrementally, can create a foundation for lasting change. Readers can draw inspiration from her ability to push past self-doubt and embrace tools that align with their unique needs.

James' Story: The Professional Seeking Balance

James Carter, a project manager at a tech startup, brought to light the challenges of managing ADHD in a high-pressure professional environment. His tendency to overcommit, lose focus during meetings, and struggle with follow-through created friction at work and stress at home. Coaching helped James develop a structured approach to task management and organization. By leveraging tools like the Eisenhower Matrix, digital planners, and mindfulness techniques, James learned to prioritize effectively and communicate more transparently with his team.

James' journey also highlighted the emotional toll of ADHD. His growth came from recognizing the importance of resilience and self-compassion. For readers, his story emphasizes that progress is not about perfection but consistently showing up and adapting to challenges.

Laura's Story: The Single Mother Juggling It All

Laura Kim's narrative as a single mother and marketing executive showcased the complexities of managing ADHD while balancing professional responsibilities and parenting. Her struggles with disorganization, work-life balance, and morning chaos at home resonated deeply. Through her sessions with a coach, Laura adopted cognitive behavioral strategies to improve prioritization, structure, and parenting routines. Key tools like habit stacking, visual reminders, and a chore tracker transformed her daily life.

Laura's story demonstrated that ADHD does not just affect individuals but also their relationships. By incorporating strategies to support her son, Ethan, Laura strengthened their bond and created a more harmonious home environment. Her journey serves as a reminder that effective ADHD management often requires a holistic approach that considers personal, professional, and familial contexts.

Nathan's Story: The Brilliant but Overfocused Engineer

Nathan Reed, a software engineer, brought a unique perspective with his experience of hyperfocus. While his ability to engage in tasks fueled his professional success, it often came at the expense of neglected responsibilities, poor nutrition, and strained relationships. Coaching helped Nathan build strategies for prioritization, organization, work-life balance, and self-care.

Nathan's inclusion of a nutrition plan was particularly impactful. Learning to meal prep, stay hydrated, and take regular breaks for meals highlighted the importance of physical health in supporting mental clarity and focus. His journey underscored the interconnectedness of wellness and productivity, inspiring readers to view ADHD management through a broader lens.

Common Themes and Lessons

Several key themes emerged across all four stories:

1. **Tailored Strategies:** Each individual's journey demonstrated the importance of finding tools and techniques that align with their unique needs and circumstances.

2. **Holistic Approaches:** Effective ADHD management extends beyond task management to include emotional resilience, relationship-building, and physical wellness.

3. **The Power of Support:** A supportive network, whether through coaching, family, or peers, is pivotal for each individual's success.

4. **Progress Over Perfection:** Setbacks were a natural part of the journey, but resilience and adaptability made each person bounce back stronger.

Readers can draw inspiration from these stories and consider how similar strategies might apply to their own lives. Sophia, James, Laura, and Nathan's courage and determination remind us that ADHD, while challenging, is not insurmountable.

Preparing for the Next Chapter: Nutrition and ADHD

As we transition to the next section on proper diet for ADHD, it's important to acknowledge the role of physical health in supporting mental and emotional well-being. Nutrition, in particular, plays a critical role in managing ADHD symptoms. As Nathan's story shows, poor dietary habits can exacerbate focus, energy levels, and mood difficulties, while intentional dietary choices can enhance cognitive function and resilience.

The following six chapters will delve into:

- The ADHD Diet: Whole Foods vs. Processed Foods
- Essential Nutrients for Brain Health
- Meal Planning and Preparation Strategies
- Hydration and Its Impact on Focus
- Supplements and ADHD: What You Need to Know
- Tracking Your Diet and Its Effects

These chapters will offer readers actionable insights into how diet can complement cognitive and behavioral strategies for managing ADHD. With the foundation laid by the stories of Sophia, James, Laura, and Nathan, the transition to a discussion on nutrition provides an opportunity to explore another vital component of holistic ADHD management.

Part III:
Nourishing Your Brain

Chapter 23

The ADHD Diet: Whole Foods vs. Processed Foods

Attention-Deficit/Hyperactivity Disorder (ADHD) is a complex neurodevelopmental disorder that affects millions of adults and children worldwide. While medication and behavioral therapy are often the primary treatments for ADHD, growing evidence suggests that diet can play a significant role in managing symptoms. This chapter will explore the impact of whole foods versus processed foods on ADHD symptoms and overall brain health.

Understanding the ADHD Brain and Nutrition

Before delving into specific dietary recommendations, it's essential to understand how nutrition affects the ADHD brain. Dr. Edward Hallowell, a leading expert in ADHD, emphasizes that "the brain is the most nutrient-dependent, energy-dependent, and toxin-vulnerable organ in the body." This means that what we eat can significantly impact brain function, particularly in individuals with ADHD.

The ADHD brain often struggles with neurotransmitter imbalances, particularly involving dopamine and norepinephrine. These neurotransmitters play crucial roles in attention, focus, and impulse control. A diet rich in whole foods can provide the necessary nutrients to support optimal neurotransmitter function, while processed foods may exacerbate imbalances.

Dr. Daniel Amen, a psychiatrist and brain disorder specialist, notes, "The food you eat can either be the safest and most powerful form of medicine or the slowest form of poison." This statement underscores the importance of dietary choices in managing ADHD symptoms.

Whole Foods: The Foundation of an ADHD-Friendly Diet

Whole foods are minimally processed and free from additives or artificial substances. They are typically nutrient-dense, providing a wide range of vitamins, minerals, and other beneficial compounds that support brain health.

1. Fruits and Vegetables

Fruits and vegetables are powerhouses of nutrition, offering a variety of benefits for individuals with ADHD. Dr. Joel Nigg, a professor of psychiatry at Oregon Health & Science University, notes that "a diet high in fruits and vegetables may help reduce inattention symptoms in children with ADHD."

Key benefits of fruits and vegetables for ADHD include:

- **Antioxidants:** These compounds protect brain cells from oxidative stress, which may be higher in individuals with ADHD.
- **Fiber:** Helps stabilize blood sugar levels, potentially reducing hyperactivity and improving focus.
- **Vitamins and minerals:** Essential for neurotransmitter production and overall brain function.

Some particularly beneficial fruits and vegetables for ADHD include:

- Berries (high in antioxidants)
- Leafy greens (rich in folate and iron)
- Citrus fruits (high in vitamin C)
- Avocados (contain healthy fats and fiber)

Dr. Drew Ramsey, a psychiatrist and author of "Eat Complete," recommends, "Aim for a rainbow of colors on your plate. Different colored fruits and vegetables provide different phytonutrients, all uniquely supporting brain health."

2. Lean Proteins

Protein is crucial for individuals with ADHD, as it provides the building blocks for neurotransmitters and helps stabilize blood sugar levels. Dr. Richard Brown, associate professor of clinical psychiatry at Columbia University, states, "Protein helps keep blood sugar levels steady, which may help control ADHD symptoms."

Good sources of lean protein include:

- Fish (especially fatty fish high in omega-3s)
- Poultry
- Eggs
- Legumes
- Nuts and seeds

Dr. Hallowell recommends starting each day with a protein-rich breakfast to set a foundation for stable energy and focus.

3. Complex Carbohydrates

Complex carbohydrates provide a steady source of energy for the brain, which is particularly important for individuals with ADHD who may struggle with energy regulation. Dr. Hallowell recommends "starting the day with a protein-rich breakfast and including complex carbohydrates to maintain steady blood sugar levels throughout the day."

Beneficial complex carbohydrates include:

- Whole grains (oats, quinoa, brown rice)
- Sweet potatoes
- Beans and lentils

Dr. David Perlmutter, a neurologist and author of "Grain Brain," cautions against excessive consumption of even whole grains, stating, "While whole grains are certainly better than refined grains, some individuals with ADHD may benefit from a lower-carbohydrate approach."

4. Healthy Fats

Healthy fats, particularly omega-3 fatty acids, are essential for brain health and have been shown to potentially improve ADHD symptoms. Dr. John Ratey, associate clinical professor of psychiatry at Harvard Medical School, notes that "omega-3s are critical for brain cell structure and function."

Good sources of healthy fats include:

- Fatty fish (salmon, mackerel, sardines)
- Nuts and seeds (especially walnuts and flaxseeds)
- Avocados
- Olive oil

Dr. Amen emphasizes the importance of omega-3s, stating, "In my experience, omega-3 fatty acid supplements are the most important supplement for ADHD."

5. Fermented Foods

Emerging research suggests a link between gut health and brain function, including ADHD symptoms. Fermented foods can support a healthy gut microbiome, potentially benefiting brain health. Dr. Uma Naidoo, a nutritional psychiatrist at Harvard Medical School, recommends incorporating fermented foods into the diet to support overall brain health.

Beneficial fermented foods include:

- Yogurt

- Kefir
- Sauerkraut
- Kimchi

Dr. Naidoo explains, "The gut-brain connection is powerful. By nurturing our gut microbiome with fermented foods, we may indirectly support our brain health and potentially alleviate some ADHD symptoms."

The Problem with Processed Foods

In contrast to whole foods, processed foods are often detrimental to individuals with ADHD. These foods are typically high in sugar, unhealthy fats, and artificial additives, which can exacerbate ADHD symptoms.

1. Added Sugars

Excessive sugar consumption can lead to rapid spikes and crashes in blood sugar levels, potentially worsening ADHD symptoms. Dr. Nigg explains, "While sugar doesn't cause ADHD, high sugar intake can lead to blood sugar fluctuations, which may worsen attention and hyperactivity in some people with ADHD."

Common sources of added sugars to avoid include:

- Sodas and sweetened beverages
- Candy and sweets
- Baked goods
- Many breakfast cereals

Dr. Mark Hyman, a functional medicine practitioner, warns, "Sugar is like a drug. It affects the same brain regions as addictive drugs and can lead to cravings and withdrawal symptoms."

2. Artificial Colors and Additives

Some studies have suggested a link between artificial food colors and preservatives and increased hyperactivity in children with ADHD. While more research is needed, many experts recommend avoiding these additives as a precautionary measure.

Dr. Benjamin Feingold, who developed the Feingold Diet for ADHD, believed that eliminating artificial colors, flavors, and preservatives could improve ADHD symptoms in some individuals. While not all experts agree on the effectiveness of this approach, many recommend minimizing intake of these additives.

Dr. Sanford Newmark, head of the Pediatric Integrative Neurodevelopmental Program at the Osher Center for Integrative Medicine, states, "While not every child with ADHD is sensitive to food additives, I've seen significant improvements in some children when these are removed from the diet."

3. Trans Fats and Unhealthy Oils

Trans fats and certain unhealthy oils can promote inflammation in the body, potentially affecting brain function. Dr. Drew Ramsey, assistant clinical professor of psychiatry at Columbia University, advises avoiding trans fats and limiting intake of omega-6 fatty acids, which are prevalent in many processed foods and can promote inflammation when consumed in excess.

Foods high in unhealthy fats to avoid include:

- Fried foods
- Many packaged snacks
- Margarine
- Processed meats

Dr. Amen notes, "Inflammation is the enemy of good brain function. Avoiding pro-inflammatory foods is crucial for managing ADHD symptoms."

4. Refined Carbohydrates

Refined carbohydrates, like those found in white bread and pasta, can cause rapid spikes in blood sugar levels, potentially leading to increased hyperactivity and decreased focus. Dr. Hallowell recommends choosing complex carbohydrates over refined ones to maintain steady energy levels throughout the day.

Dr. David Ludwig, a professor of nutrition at Harvard School of Public Health, explains, "Refined carbohydrates can lead to a roller coaster of blood sugar levels, which can be particularly problematic for individuals with ADHD."

Implementing a Whole Foods Diet for ADHD

Transitioning to a whole foods diet can be challenging, especially for individuals with ADHD who may struggle with impulse control and planning. Here are some strategies to help implement a whole foods diet:

1. Gradual Changes

Dr. Hallowell advises making gradual changes rather than attempting a complete dietary overhaul overnight. "Start by incorporating one or two new whole foods into your diet each week," he suggests. This approach can make the transition more manageable and sustainable.

2. Meal Planning and Preparation

Planning meals in advance can help individuals with ADHD stick to a whole-foods diet. Dr. Patricia Quinn, a developmental pediatrician specializing in ADHD, recommends using visual aids like meal-planning apps or calendars to organize meals for the week.

Dr. Russell Barkley, a leading ADHD researcher, adds, "Creating external structures, like meal plans, can compensate for the executive function deficits often seen in ADHD."

3. Make Healthy Foods Accessible

Keep whole foods easily accessible and visible. Dr. Ramsey suggests "creating a 'healthy snack station' in your refrigerator with pre-cut fruits and vegetables, hard-boiled eggs, and other nutrient-dense options."

4. Involve the Whole Family

For families dealing with ADHD, involving everyone in the dietary changes can increase success. Dr. Nigg recommends making meal planning and preparation a family activity to increase engagement and compliance.

5. Education and Understanding

Understanding the benefits of whole foods can increase motivation to stick with dietary changes. Dr. Naidoo suggests learning about the specific nutrients in whole foods and how they support brain health.

Specific Whole Food Recommendations for ADHD

While a balanced diet of whole foods is generally beneficial for ADHD, certain foods may be particularly helpful:

1. Fatty Fish

Rich in omega-3 fatty acids, fatty fish like salmon, mackerel, and sardines can support brain health and potentially improve ADHD symptoms. Dr. Ramsey recommends aiming for at least two servings of fatty fish per week.

2. Leafy Greens

Spinach, kale, and other leafy greens are rich in folate, iron, and antioxidants, all supporting brain health. Dr. Naidoo suggests incorporating a variety of leafy greens into daily meals.

3. Berries

Berries are high in antioxidants and can support cognitive function. Dr. Hallowell recommends adding a variety of berries to breakfast or as a snack.

4. Nuts and Seeds

Rich in healthy fats, protein, and minerals, nuts and seeds can provide sustained energy and support brain health. Dr. Brown suggests keeping a mix of nuts and seeds on hand for snacking.

5. Eggs

Eggs are a nutrient-dense food, rich in protein and choline, which is important for brain health. Dr. Quinn recommends eggs as a breakfast option to start the day with stable blood sugar levels.

The Role of Hydration

While not a food, proper hydration is crucial for brain function and can impact ADHD symptoms. Dr. Ratey notes, "Even mild dehydration can affect attention and cognitive function." He recommends drinking water throughout the day and limiting intake of sugary or caffeinated beverages.

Dr. Daniel Amen adds, "The brain is about 80% water. Staying hydrated is one of the simplest yet most effective ways to support brain function."

Potential Challenges and Solutions

Implementing a whole-food diet for ADHD can come with challenges. Here are some common issues and potential solutions:

1. Picky Eating

Many individuals with ADHD, especially children, may be picky eaters. Dr. Quinn suggests gradually introducing new foods and involving children in meal planning and preparation to increase acceptance.

Dr. Dyan Hes, a pediatrician specializing in nutrition, advises, "Don't give up. It can take up to 15-20 exposures to a new food before a child accepts it."

2. Time Constraints

Preparing whole foods can be time-consuming. Dr. Hallowell recommends batch cooking and meal prepping to save time during busy weekdays.

3. Cost Concerns

Whole foods can sometimes be more expensive than processed alternatives. To manage costs, Dr. Nigg suggests focusing on seasonal produce, buying in bulk, and utilizing frozen fruits and vegetables.

4. Sensory Issues

Some individuals with ADHD may have sensory sensitivities that make certain whole foods challenging. Dr. Brown recommends experimenting with different textures and preparation methods to find acceptable options.

The Importance of Individualization

While the general principles of a whole foods diet can benefit most individuals with ADHD, it's important to remember that everyone is different. Dr. Hallowell emphasizes, "What works for one person may not work for another. It's important to pay attention to how different foods affect your symptoms and energy levels."

Some individuals may benefit from more specific dietary approaches, such as:

- Elimination diets to identify potential food sensitivities
- Higher protein diets for those who struggle with focus and attention
- Lower carbohydrate diets for individuals who experience significant energy fluctuations

Working with a healthcare provider or registered dietitian specializing in ADHD can help curate an individualized dietary plan.

Combining Diet with Other ADHD Management Strategies

While diet can play a significant role in managing ADHD symptoms, it's most effective when combined with other treatment strategies. Dr. Quinn emphasizes, "A whole foods diet should be part of a comprehensive ADHD management plan, which may include medication, behavioral therapy, exercise, and other lifestyle modifications."

Dr. Amen adds, "Think of diet as one tool in your ADHD management toolkit. When combined with other strategies, it can be incredibly powerful."

Conclusion

The impact of diet on ADHD symptoms is an area of growing research and interest. While more studies are needed to fully understand the relationship between nutrition and ADHD, the evidence strongly suggests that a diet rich in whole foods can support brain health and potentially improve ADHD symptoms.

By focusing on nutrient-dense whole foods and minimizing processed foods, individuals with ADHD can provide their brains with the necessary nutrients for optimal function. This dietary approach, combined with other ADHD management strategies, can contribute to improved focus, reduced hyperactivity, and better overall well-being.

Dr. Hallowell concludes, "Food is medicine. By making informed choices about what we eat, we can significantly impact our brain health and ADHD symptoms. It's not about perfection, but about making better choices more often."

Remember, transitioning to a whole foods diet is a journey, not a destination. Be patient with yourself or your child as you make these changes, and celebrate small victories along the way. With time and consistency, a whole foods diet can become a sustainable and beneficial part of ADHD management.

As research in this field continues to evolve, we may gain even more insights into specific dietary strategies for ADHD. For the time being, focusing on a varied, nutrient-rich whole foods diet is a sound approach for supporting brain health and potentially alleviating ADHD symptoms.

Chapter 24

Essential Nutrients for Brain Health

The human brain is a complex organ that requires a variety of nutrients to function optimally. For individuals with ADHD, ensuring proper nutrition is particularly crucial, as certain nutrients have been shown to play a significant role in managing symptoms and supporting overall brain health. This chapter will explore the essential nutrients vital for brain health, focusing on their relevance to ADHD management.

1. Omega-3 Fatty Acids

Omega-3 fatty acids, particularly EPA (eicosapentaenoic acid) and DHA (docosahexaenoic acid), are crucial for brain health and have been extensively studied in relation to ADHD.

Dr. Edward Hallowell, a leading expert in ADHD, states, "Omega-3 fatty acids are like the building blocks for brain cells. They're essential for optimal brain function, and many individuals with ADHD are deficient in these important nutrients."

Research has shown that omega-3 supplementation can have positive effects on ADHD symptoms. A meta-analysis by Chang et al. (2018) found that omega-3 supplementation had a small but significant effect on improving ADHD symptoms, particularly inattention.

Good sources of omega-3 fatty acids include:

- Fatty fish (salmon, mackerel, sardines)
- Flaxseeds and chia seeds
- Walnuts
- Algae-based supplements (for vegetarians and vegans)

Dr. John Ratey, associate clinical professor of psychiatry at Harvard Medical School, recommends, "Aim for at least two servings of fatty fish per week, or consider a high-quality omega-3 supplement if you don't consume fish regularly."

2. Iron

Iron plays a crucial role in producing dopamine, a neurotransmitter often implicated in ADHD. Iron deficiency has been associated with more severe ADHD symptoms in some studies.

An integrative medicine specialist, Dr. Jared Skowron, explains, "Iron is essential for dopamine production. Low iron levels can mimic ADHD symptoms, so it's important to have iron levels checked, especially in children with ADHD."

A study by Konofal et al. (2008) found that iron supplementation improved ADHD symptoms in children with low ferritin levels (a measure of iron stores).

Good sources of iron include:

- Lean red meat
- Poultry
- Fish
- Beans and lentils
- Fortified cereals
- Dark leafy greens

It's important to note that iron supplementation should only be done under medical supervision, as excessive iron can be harmful.

3. Zinc

Zinc is another mineral that has been studied regarding ADHD. It plays a role in neurotransmitter production and has been found to be deficient in some individuals with ADHD.

Dr. James Greenblatt, a functional psychiatrist specializing in ADHD, notes, "Zinc is involved in the metabolism of neurotransmitters, including dopamine. Some studies have shown that zinc supplementation can improve ADHD symptoms in individuals with zinc deficiency."

A study by Bilici et al. (2004) found that zinc supplementation reduced hyperactivity and impulsivity in children with ADHD.

Good sources of zinc include:

- Oysters
- Beef
- Pumpkin seeds
- Cashews
- Chickpeas

4. Magnesium

Magnesium is involved in over 300 biochemical reactions in the body and plays a crucial role in brain function. Some research has suggested that magnesium deficiency may be more common in individuals with ADHD.

Dr. Sandy Newmark, author of "ADHD Without Drugs," states, "Magnesium helps with relaxation and sleep, which can be beneficial for individuals with ADHD. It also plays a role in neurotransmitter function."

A study by El Baza et al. (2016) found that magnesium supplementation improved cognitive function in children with ADHD.

Good sources of magnesium include:

- Dark leafy greens
- Nuts and seeds
- Avocados
- Bananas
- Dark chocolate

5. Vitamin D

Vitamin D is crucial for brain development and function. Some studies have found a link between vitamin D deficiency and ADHD symptoms.

Dr. John Cannell, founder of the Vitamin D Council, explains, "Vitamin D acts more like a hormone than a vitamin in the body. It's involved in brain development and function, and deficiency has been associated with various neurological disorders, including ADHD."

A study by Sahin et al. (2018) found that vitamin D supplementation improved ADHD symptoms in children with vitamin D deficiency.

Sources of vitamin D include:

- Sunlight exposure
- Fatty fish
- Egg yolks
- Fortified foods
- Supplements (under medical supervision)

6. B Vitamins

The B vitamins, particularly B6, B9 (folate), and B12, are essential for brain health and neurotransmitter production.

Dr. Daniel Amen, a psychiatrist and brain disorder specialist, states, "B vitamins are crucial for brain health. They're involved in the production of neurotransmitters and help with energy metabolism in brain cells."

A study by Rucklidge et al. (2014) found that a micronutrient supplement containing B vitamins improved ADHD symptoms in adults.

Good sources of B vitamins include:

- Whole grains
- Leafy greens
- Eggs
- Lean meats
- Legumes

7. Antioxidants

Antioxidants, such as vitamins C and E, help protect brain cells from oxidative stress. Some research suggests that individuals with ADHD may have higher levels of oxidative stress.

Dr. Richard Brown, associate professor of clinical psychiatry at Columbia University, explains, "Antioxidants help protect brain cells from damage. They may be essential for individuals with ADHD, as some studies have found higher levels of oxidative stress in this population."

Good sources of antioxidants include:

- Berries
- Colorful fruits and vegetables

- Green tea
- Dark chocolate

8. Protein

While not a specific nutrient, protein is crucial for brain health as it provides the building blocks for neurotransmitters.

Dr. Hallowell states, "Starting the day with a protein-rich breakfast can help stabilize blood sugar levels and improve focus throughout the morning."

Good sources of protein include:

- Eggs
- Greek yogurt
- Lean meats
- Fish
- Legumes
- Nuts and seeds

Implementing a Brain-Healthy Diet for ADHD

While understanding the importance of these nutrients is crucial, implementing a brain-healthy diet can be challenging, especially for individuals with ADHD who may struggle with planning and organization. Here are some strategies to help incorporate these nutrients into your daily diet:

1. Meal Planning

Dr. Patricia Quinn, a developmental pediatrician specializing in ADHD, suggests, "Use visual aids like meal planning apps or calendars to organize meals for the week. This can help ensure you're including a variety of brain-healthy foods."

2. Prep in Advance

Dr. Hallowell recommends, "Spend some time on the weekend prepping meals and snacks for the week. This can make it easier to stick to a healthy eating plan when you're busy or tired."

3. Make Healthy Foods Accessible

Keep brain-healthy snacks easily accessible. Dr. Greenblatt suggests creating a "smart snack station" in your refrigerator with pre-cut fruits and vegetables, hard-boiled eggs, and nuts.

4. Gradual Changes

Dr. Newmark advises, "Don't try to overhaul your entire diet simultaneously. Start by incorporating one or two new brain-healthy foods each week."

5. Involve the Whole Family

For families dealing with ADHD, involving everyone in dietary changes can increase success. Dr. Skowron recommends making meal planning and preparation a family activity to increase engagement and compliance.

Potential Challenges and Solutions

Implementing dietary changes can come with challenges, particularly for individuals with ADHD. Here are some common issues and potential solutions:

1. Picky Eating

Many individuals with ADHD, especially children, may be picky eaters. Dr. Quinn suggests gradually introducing new foods and involving children in meal planning and preparation to increase acceptance.

2. Time Constraints

Preparing whole foods can be time-consuming. Dr. Hallowell recommends batch cooking and meal prepping to save time during busy weekdays.

3. Cost Concerns

Some brain-healthy foods can be more expensive. To manage costs, Dr. Greenblatt suggests focusing on seasonal produce, buying in bulk, and utilizing frozen fruits and vegetables.

4. Sensory Issues

Some individuals with ADHD may have sensory sensitivities that make certain foods challenging. Dr. Brown recommends experimenting with different textures and preparation methods to find acceptable options.

The Role of Supplements

While obtaining nutrients from whole foods is ideal, supplements can help ensure adequate nutrient intake, especially for individuals with dietary restrictions or deficiencies.

Dr. Amen states, "While a healthy diet should be the foundation, supplements can help fill in nutritional gaps. However, working with a healthcare provider is crucial to determine which supplements are appropriate and in what doses."

Some supplements that have shown promise for ADHD include:

1. **Omega-3 Fatty Acids:** Dr. Ratey typically recommends 1000-2000 mg of combined EPA and DHA daily for adults with ADHD.

2. **Multivitamin/Mineral Complex:** Dr. Rucklidge's research has shown benefits from a broad-spectrum micronutrient supplement for ADHD symptoms.

3. **Magnesium:** Dr. Newmark often recommends 200-400 mg of magnesium for adults with ADHD, taken in the evening to aid with sleep.

4. **Zinc:** Dr. Greenblatt suggests 15-30 mg of zinc daily but emphasizes the importance of testing for deficiency before supplementing.

5. **Iron:** Iron supplementation should only be done under medical supervision and after testing for deficiency.

It's important to note that supplements can interact with medications and have side effects, so always consult with a healthcare provider before starting any supplement regimen.

The Gut-Brain Connection

Emerging research highlights the importance of gut health for brain function, including its potential role in ADHD. The gut microbiome, the collection of microorganisms living in our digestive tract, plays a crucial role in this gut-brain connection.

Dr. Uma Naidoo, a nutritional psychiatrist at Harvard Medical School, explains, "The gut and brain are in constant communication, and the health of one can significantly impact the other. This connection may be particularly relevant for individuals with ADHD."

To support a healthy gut microbiome, consider incorporating the following into your diet:

1. **Probiotics:** Found in fermented foods like yogurt, kefir, and sauerkraut

2. **Prebiotics:** Present in foods like garlic, onions, and bananas

3. **Fiber-rich foods:** Whole grains, fruits, and vegetables

Dr. Naidoo emphasizes, "A diet rich in diverse plant foods can help support a healthy gut microbiome, which may positively impact brain function and potentially ADHD symptoms."

The Importance of Hydration

While not a nutrient per se, proper hydration is crucial for brain function and can impact ADHD symptoms. Dr. Ratey notes, "Even mild dehydration can affect attention and cognitive function."

Tips for staying hydrated include:

1. Keep a water bottle with you throughout the day
2. Set reminders to drink water regularly
3. Eat water-rich fruits and vegetables
4. Limit intake of dehydrating beverages like caffeine and alcohol

Mindful Eating and ADHD

Practicing mindful eating can be particularly beneficial for individuals with ADHD, who may struggle with impulsive eating or inattention during meals.

Dr. Lidia Zylowska, author of "The Mindfulness Prescription for Adult ADHD," explains, "Mindful eating can help individuals with ADHD become more aware of their eating habits, potentially leading to better food choices and improved attention to hunger and fullness cues."

Strategies for mindful eating include:

1. Eating without distractions (e.g., turning off the TV)
2. Chewing food thoroughly and eating slowly
3. Paying attention to the sensory experience of eating
4. Checking in with hunger and fullness levels throughout the meal

Conclusion

Nutrition plays a crucial role in brain health and can significantly impact ADHD symptoms. By focusing on essential nutrients like omega-3 fatty acids, iron, zinc, magnesium, vitamin D, B vitamins, and antioxidants, individuals with ADHD can support their brain health and potentially improve their symptoms.

Dr. Hallowell concludes, "While nutrition is not a cure for ADHD, it's a powerful tool in managing symptoms and supporting overall brain health. Combined with other treatments like medication and behavioral therapy, a brain-healthy diet can help individuals with ADHD thrive."

Everyone's nutritional needs are unique, and what works for one person may not work for another. If possible, it's essential to work with healthcare providers, including a registered dietitian, to develop a nutritional plan tailored to individual needs and preferences.

Implementing dietary changes can be challenging, especially for individuals with ADHD who may struggle with planning and organization. However, with patience, persistence, and the right strategies, it's possible to develop eating habits that support brain health and overall well-being.

As research in this field evolves, we may gain more insights into the relationship between nutrition and ADHD. For the time being, focusing on a varied, nutrient-rich whole foods diet is a sound approach for supporting brain health and potentially alleviating ADHD symptoms.

Chapter 25
Meal Planning and Preparation Strategies

Meal planning and preparation can be particularly challenging for individuals with ADHD due to difficulties with organization, time management, and maintaining focus on multi-step tasks. However, developing effective strategies can significantly improve nutrition, reduce stress, and support overall ADHD management. This chapter will explore various approaches to meal planning and preparation tailored to the unique needs of adults with ADHD.

Understanding the Challenges

Before diving into strategies, it's essential to recognize the specific challenges that individuals with ADHD may face regarding meal planning and preparation:

1. **Executive Function Difficulties:** Dr. Russell Barkley, a leading ADHD researcher, explains, "ADHD is fundamentally a disorder of self-regulation and executive function. This can make planning and following through on meal preparation particularly challenging."

2. **Time Blindness:** Many adults with ADHD struggle with time perception, making it difficult to estimate how long meal preparation will take. Dr. Ari Tuckman, a psychologist specializing in ADHD, notes, "Time blindness can lead to underestimating how long meal prep will take, resulting in rushed or incomplete meals."

3. **Impulsivity:** The tendency towards impulsivity can lead to unplanned food choices or abandoning meal preparation halfway

through. Dr. Thomas Brown, author of "Smart but Stuck," states, "Impulsivity in ADHD can manifest as difficulty sticking to a meal plan or being easily swayed by immediate food cravings."

4. **Distractibility:** Kitchen environments are full of potential distractions, from appliance noises to the temptation to multitask. Dr. Edward Hallowell, co-author of "Driven to Distraction," observes, "The kitchen can be a minefield of distractions for someone with ADHD, making it challenging to complete meal preparation efficiently."

5. **Overwhelm:** The multiple steps involved in meal planning and preparation can feel overwhelming, leading to avoidance. Dr. Stephanie Sarkis, author of "Natural Relief for Adult ADHD," explains, "The prospect of planning meals for an entire week can feel insurmountable for someone with ADHD, often leading to decision paralysis."

Considering these challenges, let's explore strategies for making meal planning and preparation more manageable and successful.

1. Simplify Your Approach

Dr. Edward Hallowell advises, "The key to success for adults with ADHD is simplifying and creating structure. This applies to meal planning as much as any other area of life."

Strategies for simplification include:

a) **Theme Nights:** Assign a theme to each night of the week (e.g., Meatless Monday, Taco Tuesday). This reduces decision fatigue and provides a framework for planning. Dr. Roberto Olivardia, a clinical psychologist specializing in ADHD, adds, "Theme nights can create a sense of routine and predictability, which can be comforting for individuals with ADHD."

b) **Capsule Meal Planning:** Create a rotating list of 10-15 favorite, easy-to-prepare meals similar to a capsule wardrobe. This limits choices while ensuring variety. Dr. Patricia Quinn, a developmental pediatrician specializing in ADHD, suggests, "Having a go-to list of familiar meals can significantly reduce the cognitive load of meal planning."

c) **The "3x3" Method:** Plan three meals you will eat thrice weekly. ADHD coach Eric Tivers suggests this approach, which reduces planning and preparation time while still providing variety. Tivers explains, "This method strikes a balance between variety and simplicity, making it manageable for many adults with ADHD."

2. Utilize Visual Tools

Visual cues can be particularly helpful for individuals with ADHD. Dr. Patricia Quinn recommends using visual planners, whether digital or physical, to map out your meals for the week.

Visual planning tools might include:

a) **Whiteboard Menu:** Keep a whiteboard in the kitchen to list the week's meals. Dr. Hallowell notes, "Having a visible reminder of your meal plan can help keep you on track and reduce decision-making in the moment."

b) **Digital Meal Planning Apps:** Apps like Mealime or Plan to Eat provide visual interfaces for meal planning and can generate shopping lists. Dr. Tuckman adds, "Digital tools can be particularly helpful for adults with ADHD who are comfortable with technology, as they can provide reminders and streamline the planning process."

c) **Visual Recipe Cards:** Create or purchase visual recipe cards that break down meals into clear, pictorial steps. Dr. Brown suggests, "Visual recipe cards can help break down the meal preparation process into manageable steps, reducing overwhelm."

3. Batch Cooking and Meal Prepping

Batch cooking can significantly reduce the daily burden of meal preparation. Dr. John Ratey, author of "Spark: The Revolutionary New Science of Exercise and the Brain," notes, "Batch cooking not only saves time but can also provide a sense of accomplishment, which is important for individuals with ADHD."

Batch cooking strategies include:

a) **Weekend Prep:** Dedicate a few hours during the weekend to prepare meals for the week. Dr. Olivardia advises, "Use the weekend when you might have more time and energy to set yourself up for success during the busy week."

b) **Double Batches:** Always make double and freeze half for future meals. Dr. Sarkis explains, "This strategy allows you to build up a freezer stash of meals, providing options for those days when cooking feels overwhelming."

c) **Ingredient Prep:** Wash and chop vegetables, cook grains, or prepare proteins in advance to speed up weekday cooking. Dr. Quinn suggests, "Breaking meal prep into smaller tasks can make the process feel more manageable and less daunting."

4. Leverage Technology

Technology can provide valuable support for meal planning and preparation. ADHD coach Nikki Kinzer suggests, "Use technology to your advantage. Set reminders, use voice assistants, and explore meal planning apps."

Helpful tech tools include:

a) **Voice Assistants:** Use Alexa, Siri, or Google Assistant to set cooking timers, add items to shopping lists, or read out recipes. Dr. Ratey notes, "Voice assistants can act as an external memory aid, helping to keep you on track during meal preparation."

b) **Meal Kit Services:** Services like HelloFresh or Blue Apron can reduce the planning burden and provide structured recipes. Dr. Hallowell adds, "Meal kit services can be a great way to build cooking skills and confidence while reducing the cognitive load of meal planning."

c) **Online Grocery Ordering:** Utilize online ordering and delivery services to avoid the distractions of in-store shopping. Dr. Tuckman explains, "Online grocery shopping can help adults with ADHD stick to their meal plan and avoid impulsive purchases."

5. Create a Structured Kitchen Environment

A well-organized kitchen can significantly reduce the cognitive load of meal preparation. Dr. Stephanie Sarkis advises, "Set up your kitchen in a way that makes sense to you. Group like items together and keep frequently used items easily accessible."

Kitchen organization strategies include:

a) **Clear Labeling:** Use a label maker to mark where items belong. Dr. Brown suggests, "Clear labeling can reduce the mental effort required to find items, making meal preparation smoother."

b) **Open Shelving:** Consider using open shelves or clear containers to keep items visible. Dr. Olivardia notes, "For many adults with ADHD, out of sight truly means out of mind. Open shelving can help keep necessary items at the forefront."

c) **Cooking Station Set-up:** Create dedicated areas for different tasks (e.g., a baking station with all necessary tools and ingredients). Dr. Quinn advises, "Having everything you need for a specific task in one place can help reduce distractions and improve efficiency."

6. Incorporate Mindfulness

Mindfulness techniques can help manage the overwhelm and distractibility often associated with meal preparation. Dr. Lidia Zylowska, author of "The Mindfulness Prescription for Adult ADHD," suggests, "Approach cooking as a mindfulness practice. Focus on the sensory experience of preparing food to stay present and engaged."

Mindful cooking strategies include:

a) **Single-Tasking:** Focus on one step at a time rather than trying to multitask. Dr. Ratey explains, "Single-tasking can help reduce overwhelm and improve the quality of your meal preparation."

b) **Sensory Engagement:** Pay attention to the ingredients' colors, smells, and textures. Dr. Zylowska notes, "Engaging your senses can help anchor your attention to the present moment, reducing mind-wandering."

c) **Breathing Exercises:** Use simple breathing techniques to refocus when distracted or overwhelmed. Dr. Hallowell suggests, "A few deep breaths can help reset your focus and calm any anxiety that may arise during meal preparation."

7. Build in Flexibility

Rigid meal plans can be discouraging when they inevitably don't work out perfectly. Dr. Roberto Olivardia recommends, "Build flexibility into your meal plan. Have some easy backup meals for days when things don't go as planned."

Flexibility strategies include:

a) **"Plan B" Meals:** Always keep ingredients for a few simple, quick meals on hand. Dr. Tuckman advises, "Having backup meals can reduce stress and ensure you still eat well even when your original plan falls through."

b) **Themed Leftover Nights:** Designate one night a week as a "leftover night" to use up extra food creatively. Dr. Sarkis notes, "This can reduce food waste and provide a built-in flexible night in your meal plan."

c) **Flexible Ingredients:** Stock versatile ingredients that can be used in multiple dishes. Dr. Quinn suggests, "Having adaptable ingredients on hand allows for improvisation when needed, which can be a strength for many adults with ADHD."

8. Make it Social

For many adults with ADHD, social interaction can increase dopamine and improve focus. Dr. Edward Hallowell suggests, "Consider making meal preparation a social activity. Cook with friends or family when possible."

Social cooking ideas include:

a) **Meal Prep Parties:** Invite friends for a group meal prep session. Dr. Ratey explains, "Social interaction can make meal prep more enjoyable and help maintain focus on the task."

b) **Family Cooking Time:** Involve family members in meal preparation, assigning age-appropriate tasks. Dr. Olivardia notes, "This can be a great way to teach children about nutrition and cooking while also making the process more engaging for adults with ADHD."

c) **Virtual Cookalongs:** Set up video calls with friends to cook the same meal together, even when apart. Dr. Brown suggests, "This can provide structure and accountability, making it more likely that you'll follow through with your meal plan."

9. Use Timers and Alarms Effectively

Time management is often a challenge for individuals with ADHD. Dr. Russell Barkley advises, "Use external time markers like timers and alarms to help manage time during meal preparation."

Timer strategies include:

a) **Prep Timers:** Set a timer for prep tasks to avoid getting lost in details. Dr. Tuckman explains, "This can help prevent hyperfocus on one aspect of meal prep at the expense of others."

b) **Cooking Timers:** Use multiple timers for different meal components. Dr. Sarkis suggests, "This can help ensure that all parts of the meal are ready simultaneously, reducing stress and improving the overall dining experience."

c) **"Wrapping Up" Alarm:** Set an alarm for when to start cleaning up and finishing the meal. Dr. Quinn notes, "This can help with transitioning from cooking to eating, which can be a challenge for some individuals with ADHD."

10. Practice Self-Compassion

It's important to remember that perfection is not the goal. Dr. Roberto Olivardia emphasizes, "Be kind to yourself. Celebrate the meals you do prepare, and don't beat yourself up over the times when things don't go as planned."

Self-compassion strategies include:

a) **Positive Self-Talk:** Acknowledge your efforts, regardless of the outcome. Dr. Hallowell advises, "Recognize that any effort towards meal planning and preparation is a step in the right direction."

b) **Learning Orientation:** View cooking mishaps as learning opportunities rather than failures. Dr. Zylowska suggests approaching cooking with curiosity and a willingness to learn rather than an expectation of perfection.

c) **Progress Over Perfection:** Focus on overall progress rather than the perfect execution of every meal. Dr. Brown notes, "Consistent effort over time is more important than getting everything right all at once."

Effective meal planning and preparation can significantly improve nutrition, reduce stress, and support overall ADHD management. Implementing strategies that address the unique challenges associated with ADHD can help individuals develop sustainable habits that make healthy eating more achievable.

Remember, the goal is progress, not perfection. Dr. Edward Hallowell encourages, "Celebrate your successes, learn from your challenges, and refine your approach. With time and practice, meal planning and preparation can become a manageable and enjoyable part of your routine."

As you implement these strategies, consider what works best for you. Everyone's ADHD manifests differently, so it may take some experimentation to find the right combination of techniques. Be patient with yourself, and don't hesitate to seek support from friends, family, or professionals when needed.

With consistent effort and the right strategies, you can overcome the challenges of meal planning and preparation. You can nourish your body and brain to manage your ADHD symptoms better and improve your overall quality of life.

Chapter 26
Hydration and Its Impact on Focus

Water is essential for life, and its importance extends beyond basic survival. Proper hydration can be crucial in managing symptoms and improving cognitive function, particularly focus and attention, for individuals with ADHD. This chapter will explore the intricate relationship between hydration and focus, specifically emphasizing its relevance to adults with ADHD.

The Brain-Water Connection

The human brain comprises approximately 75% water, highlighting hydration's critical role in cognitive function. Dr. Joshua Gowin, a neuroscientist at the University of Texas, explains, "Brain cells require a delicate balance between water and various elements to operate. When you lose too much water, that balance is disrupted, and your brain cells lose efficiency."

This loss of efficiency can manifest in various ways, including:

1. Reduced cognitive performance
2. Decreased attention span
3. Impaired short-term memory
4. Slower reaction times
5. Increased irritability and mood swings

For individuals with ADHD, who already struggle with attention and focus, even mild dehydration can exacerbate these symptoms significantly.

The Impact of Dehydration on Focus

Research has consistently shown that even mild dehydration can noticeably impact cognitive function. A British Journal of Nutrition study found that a fluid loss of just 1-2% of body weight was enough to impair cognitive performance and mood.

Dr. Caroline Edmonds, a researcher at the University of East London, notes, "Our research has shown that even mild dehydration can lead to poorer concentration, increased fatigue, and reduced cognitive abilities. These effects are particularly pronounced in tasks requiring attention, memory, and psychomotor skills."

For adults with ADHD, who often struggle with these areas, the impact of dehydration can be even more pronounced. Dr. Edward Hallowell, a leading expert in ADHD, emphasizes, "Staying properly hydrated is one of the simplest yet most effective strategies for managing ADHD symptoms, particularly when it comes to focus and attention."

The Hydration-Focus Mechanism

The link between hydration and focus can be attributed to several physiological mechanisms:

1. **Blood Flow:** Proper hydration ensures optimal blood flow to the brain, delivering essential oxygen and nutrients. Dehydration can reduce blood volume, leading to decreased blood flow and reduced cognitive function.

2. **Neurotransmitter Balance:** Water plays a crucial role in the production and balance of neurotransmitters, including dopamine and norepinephrine, which are often implicated in ADHD. Dehydration can disrupt this delicate balance, potentially exacerbating ADHD symptoms.

3. **Cellular Function:** Brain cells require adequate hydration to maintain their structure and function. Dehydration can lead to cellular shrinkage, impairing neural communication and cognitive processes.

4. **Energy Metabolism:** Water is essential for efficiently converting food into energy. Dehydration can slow down this process, leading to feelings of fatigue and reduced mental alertness.

Hydration Strategies for Adults with ADHD

Given the importance of hydration for focus and attention, implementing effective hydration strategies is crucial for adults with ADHD. Here are some practical tips:

1. **Set Reminders:** Use smartphone apps or alarms to remind you to drink water regularly throughout the day. Dr. Stephanie Sarkis, an ADHD expert, suggests, "Set reminders every hour to prompt you to take a few sips of water. This can help establish a consistent hydration habit."

2. **Use Visual Cues:** Keep a water bottle visible on your desk or in your line of sight. Dr. Russell Barkley, a leading ADHD researcher, notes, "Visual cues can be particularly effective for individuals with ADHD, serving as constant reminders to stay hydrated."

3. **Flavor Your Water:** If plain water is unappealing, add natural flavors like lemon, cucumber, or berries. Dr. John Ratey, associate clinical professor of psychiatry at Harvard Medical School, advises, "Making water more palatable can increase your likelihood of drinking it regularly."

4. **Track Your Intake:** Use a water tracking app or a marked water bottle to monitor your daily water intake. This can help you ensure you are meeting your hydration goals.

5. **Eat Water-Rich Foods:** Incorporate foods with high water content, such as cucumbers, watermelon, and lettuce, into your diet. These can contribute to your overall hydration levels.

6. **Create a Routine:** Associate drinking water with specific daily activities, such as taking medication or checking emails. This can help make hydration a habitual part of your routine.

7. **Limit Dehydrating Beverages:** Reduce consumption of caffeine and alcohol, which can have a diuretic effect. If you do consume these beverages, compensate by increasing your water intake.

The Role of Electrolytes

While water is crucial for hydration, electrolytes also play a vital role in maintaining proper fluid balance. Dr. Uma Naidoo, a nutritional psychiatrist at Harvard Medical School, explains, "Electrolytes help regulate nerve and muscle function, hydrate the body, balance blood acidity and pressure, and help rebuild damaged tissue."

For adults with ADHD, maintaining proper electrolyte balance can contribute to improved focus and cognitive function. Consider incorporating electrolyte-rich foods into your diet, such as:

1. Bananas (potassium)
2. Yogurt (calcium)
3. Spinach (magnesium)
4. Coconut water (multiple electrolytes)

In some cases, electrolyte supplements may be beneficial, especially during intense physical activity or hot weather. However, it is important to consult with a healthcare professional before starting any supplementation regimen.

Hydration and Medication Interactions

For adults with ADHD who are taking medication, proper hydration is even more critical. Many ADHD medications, particularly stimulants, can have side effects that impact hydration levels. Dr. William Dodson, a psychiatrist specializing in ADHD, notes, "Stimulant medications can sometimes cause dry mouth and increased urination, potentially leading to dehydration if not properly managed."

You must know these potential interactions and adjust your hydration strategies accordingly. This may involve:

1. Increasing water intake when taking medication
2. Timing water consumption around medication doses
3. Monitoring for signs of dehydration more closely
4. Discussing hydration concerns with your healthcare provider

Overcoming Hydration Challenges

Despite understanding the importance of hydration, many adults with ADHD may struggle to maintain consistent water intake. Common challenges include:

1. **Forgetfulness:** The tendency to become engrossed in tasks and forget to drink water
2. **Time Blindness:** Difficulty perceiving the passage of time, leading to long periods without hydration

3. **Sensory Issues:** Discomfort with certain water temperatures or textures
4. **Hyperfocus:** Becoming so focused on a task that basic needs like hydration are ignored

To overcome these challenges, Dr. Thomas Brown, a clinical psychologist specializing in ADHD, suggests, "It's important to create systems and routines that make hydration as automatic as possible. This might involve setting alarms, using visual cues, or enlisting the help of friends or family members to provide reminders."

The Long-Term Benefits of Proper Hydration

While the immediate effects of hydration on focus and attention are significant, proper hydration also has enormous long-term benefits. Dr. Natalia Dmitrieva, a heart researcher at the National Institutes of Health, has studied the long-term effects of chronic mild dehydration. Her research suggests that consistent, adequate hydration may help reduce the risk of chronic diseases and contribute to healthier aging.

For adults with ADHD, who may be at increased risk for certain health complications, maintaining proper hydration throughout life can be an important part of an overall health and wellness strategy.

Hydration and Cognitive Performance

Recent studies have shed light on the specific ways in which hydration affects cognitive performance, particularly in areas that are often challenging for individuals with ADHD. A study conducted at the University of East London found that participants who drank water before performing cognitive tasks showed improved performance in visual attention and memory tasks.

Dr. Edmonds, who led the study, explains, "Our findings suggest that even a small amount of water can significantly improve cognitive performance, particularly in tasks that require sustained attention and working memory – areas often problematic for individuals with ADHD."

Another study published in the journal Frontiers in Human Neuroscience found that mild dehydration (1-2% of body weight) decreased performance in tasks requiring attention, psychomotor skills, and immediate memory. The researchers noted that these effects were more pronounced in individuals who were already experiencing cognitive challenges, suggesting that adults with ADHD may be particularly vulnerable to the cognitive effects of dehydration.

Hydration and Mood Regulation

In addition to impacting cognitive function, hydration also plays a crucial role in mood regulation—another area that can be challenging for adults with ADHD. A study published in the Journal of Nutrition found that mild dehydration was associated with decreased mood, increased perception of task difficulty, and higher levels of anxiety and fatigue.

Dr. Harris Lieberman, a U.S. Army Research Institute of Environmental Medicine research psychologist and one of the study's authors, notes, "Even mild dehydration can alter a person's mood, energy level, and ability to think clearly. These effects may be more pronounced in individuals who are already struggling with mood regulation, such as those with ADHD."

For adults with ADHD, who often experience emotional dysregulation as part of their symptom profile, maintaining proper hydration can be an essential strategy for mood management.

Practical Tips for Increasing Water Intake

Given the importance of hydration for cognitive function and mood regulation, adults with ADHD must develop strategies for increasing their water intake. Here are some additional practical tips:

1. **Use a Smart Water Bottle:** Consider investing in a smart water bottle that tracks your water intake and sends reminders to drink. These high-tech solutions can be particularly appealing to adults with ADHD who enjoy gadgets and technology.

2. **Gamify Your Hydration:** Turn hydration into a game or challenge. Set daily goals and reward yourself for meeting them. This can help make the process of staying hydrated more engaging and motivating.

3. **Pair Water with Other Habits:** Whenever you check your phone or social media, sip water. This can help you associate hydration with an activity you will likely do frequently throughout the day.

4. **Use Hydration Apps:** Numerous apps are designed to help you track and increase your water intake. Many of these apps offer features like customized reminders, progress tracking, and even social sharing to keep you motivated.

5. **Experiment with Temperature:** Some people drink more water at a specific temperature. Try cold, room-temperature, and warm water to discover your preference.

6. **Create a Hydration Station:** Set up a dedicated area in your home or office with various water options – plain water, infused water, sparkling water, etc. Having multiple options readily available can make hydration more appealing.

7. **Use Straws:** Some people find that they drink more water when using a straw. Consider keeping reusable straws with your water bottles.

Hydration and Sleep

Proper hydration is also crucial for healthy sleep patterns, which are often disrupted in adults with ADHD. While it's important not to drink too much water close to bedtime to avoid nighttime awakenings, maintaining good hydration throughout the day can contribute to better sleep quality.

A clinical psychologist and sleep specialist, Dr. Michael Breus, explains, "Dehydration can lead to a dry mouth and nasal passages, which may cause disruptive snoring and less restful sleep. Additionally, even mild dehydration can cause feelings of fatigue and lethargy, making it harder to maintain a consistent sleep schedule."

For adults with ADHD, who often struggle with sleep issues, focusing on proper hydration throughout the day can be an important part of a comprehensive sleep hygiene strategy.

Hydration in Different Environments

It's important to note that hydration needs can vary depending on environmental factors and activity levels. Adults with ADHD should be particularly mindful of their hydration in the following situations:

1. **Office Environments:** Air-conditioned offices can be dehydrating. Keep a water bottle at your desk and set reminders to drink regularly.

2. **During Exercise:** Increase water intake before, during, and after physical activity to replace fluids lost through sweat.

3. **In Hot Weather:** Heat increases the body's water needs. Be extra vigilant about hydration during the summer months or in hot climates.

4. **While Traveling:** Air travel, in particular, can be dehydrating. Bring an empty water bottle to fill after passing through security, and drink water regularly during flights.

5. **In High Altitudes:** Higher altitudes can increase fluid loss through respiration and urination. Increase water intake when visiting or living in high-altitude areas.

Conclusion

The impact of hydration on focus and attention is clear, and for adults with ADHD, proper hydration can be a powerful tool in managing symptoms and improving cognitive function. By understanding the mechanisms behind this connection and implementing effective hydration strategies, individuals with ADHD can harness the power of proper hydration to enhance their focus, attention, and overall well-being.

Remember, staying hydrated is not just about drinking water when thirsty. It's about maintaining consistent hydration throughout the day to support optimal brain function. As Dr. Hallowell aptly puts it, "Hydration is one of the simplest yet most powerful interventions we have for managing ADHD symptoms. It's a strategy accessible to everyone and can make a real difference in daily functioning."

Prioritizing hydration and making it a central part of your ADHD management strategy is an important step toward improved focus, better symptom control, and enhanced overall health. While it may seem like a small change, the cumulative effects of proper hydration can be significant, contributing to better cognitive performance, improved mood regulation, and a higher quality of life.

As with any aspect of ADHD management, it's important to approach hydration as part of a comprehensive strategy that may include medication, therapy, lifestyle modifications, and other interventions as recommended by your healthcare provider. By combining proper hydration with other evidence-based approaches to ADHD management, you can create a powerful toolkit for navigating the challenges of ADHD and maximizing your potential for success and well-being.

Chapter 27

Supplements and ADHD: What You Need to Know

Attention-Deficit/Hyperactivity Disorder (ADHD) is a complex neurodevelopmental disorder that affects millions of adults worldwide. While medication and behavioral therapies are often the primary treatments for ADHD, many individuals seek complementary approaches to manage their symptoms. One such approach is the use of dietary supplements. This chapter will explore the role of supplements in ADHD management, discussing the potential benefits, risks, and what current research says about their effectiveness.

Understanding Supplements and ADHD

Before delving into specific supplements, it's important to understand what we mean by "supplements" in the context of ADHD management. Dietary supplements contain vitamins, minerals, herbs, amino acids, or other substances intended to supplement the diet. They are not medications intended to treat, diagnose, prevent, or cure diseases.

Dr. Edward Hallowell, a leading expert in ADHD, explains, "While supplements can be beneficial for some individuals with ADHD, they should not be seen as a replacement for proven treatments like medication and behavioral therapy. Instead, they can be part of a comprehensive approach to managing ADHD symptoms."

The Potential Role of Supplements in ADHD Management

The interest in supplements for ADHD stems from the understanding that certain nutrients play crucial roles in brain function and neurotransmitter production. Some researchers hypothesize that deficiencies in these nutrients may contribute to ADHD symptoms. Therefore, supplementing with these nutrients might help alleviate symptoms.

Dr. James Greenblatt, a functional psychiatrist specializing in ADHD, notes, "While the research is still evolving, we've seen promising results with certain supplements in improving attention, reducing impulsivity, and supporting overall cognitive function in individuals with ADHD."

Key Supplements Studied for ADHD

1. Omega-3 Fatty Acids

Numerous studies have examined omega-3 fatty acids, particularly EPA (eicosapentaenoic acid) and DHA (docosahexaenoic acid), regarding ADHD. These essential fats play a crucial role in brain structure and function.

A meta-analysis by Chang et al. (2018) found that omega-3 supplementation had a small but significant improvement in ADHD symptoms, particularly inattention. Dr. John Ratey, associate clinical professor of psychiatry at Harvard Medical School, explains, "Omega-3s are crucial for brain health. They're involved in neurotransmitter function and can help reduce inflammation in the brain, which may contribute to ADHD symptoms."

Recommended dosage: Most studies have used doses ranging from 500 mg to 2000 mg of combined EPA and DHA daily. However, consulting with a healthcare provider for personalized recommendations is important.

2. Zinc

Zinc is an essential mineral that plays a role in neurotransmitter production and regulation. Some studies have found lower zinc levels in individuals with ADHD.

A study by Bilici et al. (2004) found that zinc supplementation reduced hyperactivity and impulsivity in children with ADHD. Dr. Greenblatt notes, "Zinc is involved in the metabolism of neurotransmitters, including dopamine. Some individuals with ADHD may benefit from zinc supplementation, particularly if they have a deficiency."

Recommended dosage: The typical study dose is 15-30 mg daily. However, zinc can be toxic in high doses, so it's crucial to have levels tested before supplementing.

3. Iron

Iron is crucial for dopamine production, a neurotransmitter often implicated in ADHD. Some research has found a link between iron deficiency and ADHD symptoms.

A study by Konofal et al. (2008) found that iron supplementation improved ADHD symptoms in children with low ferritin levels (a measure of iron stores). Dr. Hallowell explains, "Iron deficiency can mimic ADHD symptoms. It's important to check iron levels, especially in children with ADHD."

Recommended dosage: Iron supplementation should only be done under medical supervision, as excessive iron can be harmful.

4. Magnesium

Magnesium is involved in over 300 biochemical reactions in the body and plays a crucial role in brain function. Some research suggests that magnesium deficiency may be more common in individuals with ADHD.

A study by El Baza et al. (2016) found that magnesium supplementation improved cognitive function in children with ADHD. Dr. Sandy

Newmark, author of "ADHD Without Drugs," states, "Magnesium helps with relaxation and sleep, which can be beneficial for individuals with ADHD. It also plays a role in neurotransmitter function."

Recommended dosage: Typical doses range from 200 to 400 mg daily for adults. However, as with all supplements, it's important to consult a healthcare provider before starting supplementation.

5. Vitamin D

Vitamin D is crucial for brain development and function. Some studies have found a link between vitamin D deficiency and ADHD symptoms.

A study by Sahin et al. (2018) found that vitamin D supplementation improved ADHD symptoms in children with vitamin D deficiency. Dr. John Cannell, founder of the Vitamin D Council, explains, "Vitamin D acts more like a hormone than a vitamin in the body. It's involved in brain development and function, and deficiency has been associated with various neurological disorders, including ADHD."

Recommended dosage: Vitamin D dosage can vary widely based on individual needs and current levels. It's important to have vitamin D levels tested before supplementing.

6. B Vitamins

The B vitamins, particularly B6, B9 (folate), and B12, are essential for brain health and neurotransmitter production.

A study by Rucklidge et al. (2014) found that a micronutrient supplement containing B vitamins improved ADHD symptoms in adults. Dr. Daniel Amen, a psychiatrist and brain disorder specialist, states, "B vitamins are crucial for brain health. They're involved in the production of neurotransmitters and help with energy metabolism in brain cells."

Recommended dosage: B vitamin needs can vary widely. A high-quality B-complex supplement or a multivitamin containing B vitamins is often recommended.

7. L-Theanine

L-Theanine is an amino acid found in tea leaves. It's known for its calming effects and ability to improve focus without causing drowsiness.

While research on L-Theanine specifically for ADHD is limited, some studies have shown promising results for improving attention and reducing anxiety. Dr. Greenblatt notes, "L-Theanine can be particularly helpful for individuals with ADHD who also struggle with anxiety. It can promote a state of calm focus."

Recommended dosage: Typical doses range from 100-200 mg, taken up to twice daily.

8. Phosphatidylserine

Phosphatidylserine is a phospholipid that's crucial for cognitive function. It's involved in cell signaling, particularly in the brain.

Some studies have shown improvements in ADHD symptoms with phosphatidylserine supplementation, particularly in combination with omega-3 fatty acids. Dr. Hallowell explains, "Phosphatidylserine can help support memory and cognitive function. It may be particularly beneficial for adults with ADHD who are also experiencing age-related cognitive decline."

Recommended dosage: Typical doses range from 100-400mg daily.

9. Ginkgo Biloba

Ginkgo Biloba is an herb used for centuries in traditional medicine. It's known for potentially improving blood flow to the brain and enhancing cognitive function.

A study by Uebel-von Sandersleben et al. (2014) found that Ginkgo Biloba improved ADHD symptoms in children. Dr. Greenblatt comments, "While more research is needed, Ginkgo Biloba shows promise in improving attention and reducing impulsivity in some individuals with ADHD."

Recommended dosage: Typical doses range from 120 to 240 mg daily, but it's crucial to consult with a healthcare provider before use, as Ginkgo can interact with certain medications.

10. Rhodiola Rosea

Rhodiola Rosea is an adaptogenic herb that may help the body manage stress more effectively. Some studies suggest it may improve focus and reduce fatigue.

Dr. Amen notes, "Rhodiola can be particularly helpful for adults with ADHD who struggle with stress-induced cognitive impairment. It may help improve mental performance under stress."

Recommended dosage: Typical doses range from 200 to 400 mg daily, but as with all supplements, it's important to consult with a healthcare provider before use.

Potential Risks and Considerations

While supplements can offer potential benefits, it's crucial to approach their use with caution. Dr. Russell Barkley, a leading ADHD researcher, warns, "Supplements are not regulated like medications. The quality and purity of supplements can vary widely, and some may interact with medications or have side effects."

Some important considerations include:

1. **Quality:** Choose supplements from reputable manufacturers that undergo third-party testing.
2. **Interactions:** Some supplements can interact with ADHD medications or other medications you may be taking. Always consult with your healthcare provider before starting any new supplement.

3. **Overdosing:** Some vitamins and minerals can be harmful in high doses. For example, excessive iron or zinc intake can be toxic.

4. **Individual Differences:** What works for one person may not work for another. Working with a healthcare provider is important to determine what's best for your individual needs.

5. **Cost:** High-quality supplements can be expensive. It's important to weigh the potential benefits against the cost.

6. **Expectations:** Supplements are not a cure for ADHD. They may help manage symptoms in some individuals. Still, they do not replace proven treatments like medication and behavioral therapy.

The Importance of a Holistic Approach

While supplements can help manage ADHD, they are most effective when used as part of a comprehensive treatment plan. Dr. Hallowell emphasizes, "The most effective approach to managing ADHD involves a combination of strategies, including medication when appropriate, behavioral interventions, lifestyle modifications, and possibly supplements."

A holistic approach to ADHD management might include:

1. **Proper Nutrition:** A balanced diet rich in whole foods provides many important nutrients for brain health.

2. **Regular Exercise:** Physical activity has been shown to improve ADHD symptoms and overall cognitive function.

3. **Adequate Sleep:** Good sleep habits are crucial for managing ADHD symptoms.

4. **Stress Management:** Techniques like mindfulness and meditation can help manage stress and improve focus.

5. **Behavioral Strategies:** Techniques like time management, organization skills, and cognitive-behavioral therapy can effectively manage ADHD symptoms.

6. **Medication:** For many individuals with ADHD, medication is an important part of treatment.

7. **Supplements:** Certain supplements may provide additional support when used under medical supervision.

Dr. Amen notes, "The goal is to create an internal and external environment that supports optimal brain function. Supplements can be one piece of that puzzle, but they're not the whole picture."

The Future of Supplement Research in ADHD

Research into the role of supplements in ADHD management is ongoing. Dr. Greenblatt predicts, "As we gain a better understanding of the neurobiological underpinnings of ADHD, we may be able to develop more targeted nutritional interventions. Personalized medicine, based on an individual's unique biochemistry, is likely to play a bigger role in the future of ADHD treatment."

Some promising areas of research include:

1. **Gut-Brain Connection:** Emerging research explores the link between gut health and ADHD symptoms. Probiotics and prebiotics may play a role in future ADHD management strategies.

2. **Personalized Nutrient Testing:** Advanced testing methods may allow for more targeted supplementation based on an individual's specific deficiencies.

3. **Combination Therapies:** Research is exploring how different combinations of nutrients might work synergistically to improve ADHD symptoms.

4. **Long-Term Effects:** More long-term studies are needed to understand the effects of supplement use over time in individuals with ADHD.

Implementing a Supplement Regimen

If you are considering incorporating supplements into your ADHD management plan, here are some steps to follow:

1. **Consult with a Healthcare Provider:** Before starting any supplement regimen, it's crucial to consult with a healthcare provider who is knowledgeable about ADHD and nutritional approaches. They can help you determine which supplements might be most beneficial for your specific situation and can monitor for any potential side effects or interactions.

2. **Get Tested:** Consider getting tested for nutrient deficiencies. This can help guide your supplement choices and ensure you're addressing specific needs.

3. **Start Slowly:** When introducing new supplements, start with one at a time and at a lower dose. This allows you to monitor for any effects or side effects more easily.

4. **Keep a Journal:** Track your symptoms, mood, and any changes you notice when taking supplements. This can help you and your healthcare provider determine what's working and what's not.

5. **Be Patient:** The effects of nutritional interventions can take time to manifest. Give any new supplement regimen at least a few weeks before evaluating its effectiveness.

6. **Regular Review:** Review your supplement regimen with your healthcare provider. Your needs may change over time, and it is important to adjust your approach.

7. **Don't Neglect Other Aspects of ADHD Management:** Remember that supplements are part of a comprehensive ADHD management plan. Continue to focus on other important aspects like medication (if prescribed), therapy, exercise, and sleep hygiene.

Supplements can offer potential benefits for some individuals with ADHD, but they are not a one-size-fits-all solution. The decision to use supplements should be made in consultation with a healthcare provider, considering individual needs, potential risks, and overall treatment goals.

Dr. Hallowell concludes, "While the idea of a 'natural' treatment for ADHD is appealing, it's important to approach supplement use with a balanced perspective. They can be a helpful tool in managing ADHD symptoms for some people, but they're not a magic bullet. A comprehensive approach addressing all health and well-being aspects is key to effectively managing ADHD."

Remember, managing ADHD is a journey; what works best can vary from person to person. Be patient with yourself as you explore different strategies, including the potential use of supplements. Keep track of any changes in your symptoms, both positive and negative, and communicate openly with your healthcare provider.

By combining evidence-based treatments, lifestyle modifications, and potentially beneficial supplements under proper medical supervision, you can develop a personalized approach to managing your ADHD symptoms and improving your overall quality of life. The key is to remain informed, be proactive in your health management, and work closely with healthcare professionals to find the most effective combination of strategies for your unique needs.

As research in this field evolves, stay informed about new developments and be open to adjusting your approach as new evidence emerges. With patience, persistence, and a comprehensive approach to ADHD management, you can work toward better focus, improved productivity, and enhanced overall well-being.

Chapter 28

Tracking Your Diet and Its Effects

Tracking your diet and its effects is crucial to understanding how nutrition impacts your ADHD symptoms and overall well-being. This chapter will explore the importance of dietary tracking, various methods for doing so effectively, and how to interpret the results to make informed decisions about your diet and ADHD management.

The Importance of Dietary Tracking

Dr. Edward Hallowell, a leading expert in ADHD, emphasizes, "What you eat can significantly impact your ADHD symptoms. Keeping track of your diet helps you identify patterns and connect between what you consume and how you feel."

Tracking your diet can provide several benefits:

1. **Increased awareness:** Recording what you eat makes you more conscious of your food choices and eating habits.

2. **Identification of triggers:** Tracking can help you pinpoint foods that may exacerbate your ADHD symptoms.

3. **Recognition of beneficial foods:** You can identify foods that improve your focus and energy levels.

4. **Accountability:** Keeping a food diary can help you meet your nutritional goals.

5. **Better communication with healthcare providers:** Detailed dietary information can help your doctor or nutritionist provide more tailored advice.

Methods of Dietary Tracking

There are various ways to track your diet, from traditional pen-and-paper methods to high-tech apps. The key is to find a method that works for you and that you can consistently maintain.

1. Paper Food Diary

A simple notebook can be an effective tool for tracking your diet. Dr. Russell Barkley, a prominent ADHD researcher, notes, "For some individuals with ADHD, the physical act of writing can help reinforce memory and increase engagement with the tracking process."

Pros:
- No technology required
- Can be personalized to your needs
- Portable and always accessible

Cons:
- Requires consistent effort to maintain
- Can be easy to forget or misplace
- Doesn't provide automatic analysis of nutritional content

How to use:
- Write down everything you eat and drink, including portion sizes
- Note the time of each meal or snack
- Include any supplements you take
- Record how you feel after eating, particularly in terms of ADHD symptoms

2. Smartphone Apps

There are numerous apps designed for dietary tracking. Popular options include MyFitnessPal, LoseIt, and Cronometer.

Dr. Stephanie Sarkis, an ADHD expert, suggests, "Apps can be particularly helpful for individuals with ADHD as they often provide reminders and make it easy to log meals quickly."

Pros:
- Easy to use and always with you
- Many apps have large databases of foods with nutritional information
- Can provide analysis of nutrient intake
- Often include features like barcode scanning for packaged foods

Cons:
- Requires consistent access to a smartphone
- Some apps may have a learning curve
- Privacy concerns with data sharing

How to use:
- Choose an app that feels intuitive to you
- Set reminders to log your meals
- Use the barcode scanner for packaged foods
- Take advantage of any analysis tools the app offers

3. Photography Method

Taking photos of your meals can be a quick and visual way to track your diet.

Dr. John Ratey, associate clinical professor of psychiatry at Harvard Medical School, notes, "Visual documentation can be particularly effective for individuals with ADHD who process information better visually."

Pros:
- Quick and easy
- Provides a visual record of portion sizes and food choices
- Can be combined with other tracking methods

Cons:
- Does not provide detailed nutritional information
- May be easy to forget, especially for snacks or drinks

How to use:
- Take a photo of everything you eat and drink
- Try to include a size reference (like a coin) for portion estimation
- Consider using a dedicated app for food photography, or simply use your phone's camera

4. Voice Recording

For those who find writing or typing challenging, voice recording can be an alternative method.

Dr. Thomas Brown, a clinical psychologist specializing in ADHD, suggests, "Voice recording can be a quick and easy way to capture dietary information, especially for those who struggle with written tracking."

Pros:
- Quick and easy
- Can capture more detailed information about meals and how you feel
- Useful for those who prefer speaking to writing

Cons:
- Requires transcription for analysis
- May feel awkward in public settings

How to use:
- Use your phone's voice recorder or a dedicated app
- Describe what you ate, when, and how you felt afterward
- Consider transcribing your recordings at the end of each day or week for easier analysis

5. Wearable Devices

Some wearable devices, like Fitbit or Apple Watch models, offer features for tracking food intake.

Dr. William Dodson, a psychiatrist specializing in ADHD, notes, "Wearable devices can provide a comprehensive picture of health by combining dietary information with data on physical activity and sleep patterns."

Pros:
- Integrates dietary tracking with other health metrics
- Often syncs with smartphone apps for easy viewing and analysis
- Can provide reminders to log meals

Cons:
- Can be expensive
- May have limited food databases compared to dedicated nutrition apps

How to use:
- Follow the device's instructions for logging meals
- Take advantage of any integration with smartphone apps
- Use in conjunction with other tracking methods for more detailed information

What to Track

Regardless of the method you choose, it's important to track certain key elements:

1. **Food and Drink Consumed:** Record everything you eat and drink, including snacks and beverages.

2. **Portion Sizes:** Estimate or measure portion sizes to get an accurate intake picture.

3. **Timing of Meals:** Note when you eat, as meal timing can affect ADHD symptoms.

4. **Supplements:** Record any vitamins or supplements you take.

5. **ADHD Symptoms:** Track your symptoms throughout the day, noting any changes in focus, energy levels, or mood.

6. **Sleep:** Record your sleep patterns, as sleep can significantly impact ADHD symptoms and is often affected by diet.

7. **Physical Activity:** Note any exercise or significant physical activity that can affect diet and ADHD symptoms.

8. **Medications:** If you are taking ADHD medications, record when you take them and any noticeable effects.

Dr. Uma Naidoo, a nutritional psychiatrist at Harvard Medical School, emphasizes, "The interplay between diet, sleep, physical activity, and ADHD symptoms is complex. Tracking all these elements can provide valuable insights into managing your ADHD."

Analyzing Your Dietary Tracking

Once you have collected data for a few weeks, it's time to analyze the information. Here are some steps to help you make sense of your tracking:

1. Look for Patterns

Dr. Hallowell suggests, "Review your logs weekly to identify any patterns. Do certain foods seem to coincide with better focus or more severe ADHD symptoms?"

Consider:

- Do you notice improved focus after meals rich in protein?
- Are there any foods that seem to trigger hyperactivity or inattention?
- How does your symptom management change when you eat more whole foods versus processed foods?

2. Assess Nutrient Intake

If you are using an app that provides nutritional analysis, review your intake of key nutrients important for ADHD management.

Dr. Greenblatt advises, "Pay particular attention to your intake of omega-3 fatty acids, iron, zinc, and magnesium, as these nutrients are often beneficial for individuals with ADHD."

3. Evaluate Meal Timing and Frequency

Dr. Barkley notes, "For many individuals with ADHD, eating smaller, more frequent meals can help maintain steady energy levels and improve focus."

Consider:

- How do you feel when eating three large meals versus several smaller ones?
- Is there a particular time of day when you struggle most with ADHD symptoms? How does this relate to your eating patterns?

4. Examine Sleep Patterns

Dr. Ratey emphasizes, "Sleep and diet are intimately connected, and both can significantly impact ADHD symptoms."

Look for connections between your diet and sleep patterns:

- Do certain foods or eating times seem to affect your sleep quality?
- How does your sleep affect your food choices the next day?

5. Consider Hydration

Dr. Naidoo suggests, "Don't overlook the importance of hydration. Even mild dehydration can exacerbate ADHD symptoms."

Analyze your fluid intake:

- Are you consistently drinking enough water throughout the day?
- Do you notice any changes in your symptoms based on your hydration levels?

6. Reflect on Overall Well-being

Beyond specific ADHD symptoms, consider how different dietary patterns affect your overall sense of well-being.

Dr. Sarkis advises, "Pay attention to your energy levels, mood, and general sense of health. These factors can all impact your ability to manage ADHD symptoms."

Making Adjustments Based on Your Tracking

Once you have analyzed your dietary tracking, you can start making informed adjustments to your diet. Here are some steps to consider:

1. Gradual Changes

Dr. Hallowell recommends, "Make one small change at a time. This allows you to see the effects more clearly and makes the changes more sustainable."

For example:

- If you feel more focused after protein-rich breakfasts, try incorporating more protein into your morning meal for a week and observe the effects.
- If you suspect that a particular food might trigger symptoms, try eliminating it for a few weeks and see if you notice any improvements.

2. Consult with Professionals

Dr. Greenblatt emphasizes, "While self-experimentation can be valuable, it's important to consult with healthcare professionals, particularly when making significant dietary changes."

Consider sharing your tracking results with the following:

- Your primary care physician
- A psychiatrist specializing in ADHD
- A registered dietitian familiar with ADHD

3. Be Patient

Dr. Brown advises, "Dietary changes can take time to show effects. Give each change at least a few weeks before deciding whether it's helpful."

4. Stay Flexible

Dr. Ratey notes, "What works for you may change over time. Continue tracking even after you find a diet that works well, and be open to making adjustments as needed."

5. Consider External Factors

Dr. Barkley reminds us, "Remember that diet is just one factor affecting ADHD symptoms. Consider how other stress, sleep, and exercise might affect dietary changes."

Overcoming Challenges in Dietary Tracking

While dietary tracking can be incredibly valuable, it can also present challenges, particularly for individuals with ADHD. Here are some common obstacles and strategies to overcome them:

1. Forgetfulness

Challenge: You might forget to log meals or snacks, especially when busy or distracted.

Strategies:

- Set reminders on your phone for after-meal times
- Keep your tracking tool (whether a notebook or phone) visible during meals
- Make tracking part of your mealtime routine, like brushing your teeth after eating

2. Inconsistency

Challenge: You might track diligently for a few days, then stop for a while.

Strategies:

- Start with a manageable goal, like tracking one meal a day
- Use a habit-tracking app to motivate yourself to maintain a streak
- Find an accountability partner who can check in on your tracking progress

3. Overwhelm

Challenge: The idea of tracking everything you eat might feel overwhelming.

Strategies:

- Start simple: just write down the main components of your meals
- Use a method that feels easiest for you, even if it's just taking photos of your meals
- Remember that imperfect tracking is better than no tracking at all

4. Difficulty Estimating Portion Sizes

Challenge: You might struggle to estimate how much you are eating accurately.

Strategies:

- Use common objects for comparison (e.g., a deck of cards is about the size of a 3-ounce serving of meat)
- Consider using a food scale for a week to get a better sense of portion sizes
- Use measuring cups and spoons when possible

5. Time Constraints

Challenge: You might feel like you don't have time to track your diet.

Strategies:

- Choose a quick method like taking photos or using voice recording
- Set aside a specific time each day to update your food log
- Remember that even partial tracking can provide valuable insights

6. Hyperfocus on Tracking

Challenge: You might become overly focused on tracking, leading to stress or obsessive behaviors.

Strategies:

- Set boundaries for how much time you will spend on tracking each day
- Remember that tracking is a tool, not a goal in itself
- If tracking is causing significant stress, consult with a healthcare provider

Dr. Sarkis advises, "If tracking becomes a source of stress rather than a helpful tool, it's important to reassess your approach. The goal is to gain insights, not to create additional anxiety."

Long-term Benefits of Dietary Tracking

While dietary tracking requires effort, the long-term benefits can be significant. Dr. Hallowell notes, "Consistent tracking over time can lead to a deeper understanding of your body and how to manage your ADHD symptoms through nutrition best."

Some potential long-term benefits include:

1. **Improved Symptom Management:** By identifying dietary patterns that work best for you, you can potentially reduce the severity of your ADHD symptoms.

2. **Better Overall Health:** Paying attention to what you eat often leads to healthier food choices overall.

3. **Increased Self-awareness:** Tracking can help you become more attuned to your body's signals and needs.

4. **Enhanced Communication with Healthcare Providers:** Detailed dietary information can help your healthcare team provide more personalized treatment recommendations.

5. **Greater Sense of Control:** Understanding how diet affects your symptoms can give you greater control over your ADHD management.

Tracking your diet and its effects on your ADHD symptoms is a powerful tool for self-understanding and improved symptom management. While it may seem daunting initially, finding and consistently using a tracking method that works for you can provide valuable insights into how nutrition impacts your ADHD.

Remember, there is no one-size-fits-all approach to diet and ADHD. What works for one person may only work for one person. The goal of tracking is to discover what works best for you.

Dr. Naidoo concludes, "Dietary tracking is a journey of self-discovery. Be patient with yourself, celebrate small victories, and don't hesitate to seek support when needed. With time and persistence, you can develop a deeper understanding of how your diet affects your ADHD symptoms and overall well-being."

As you progress with your dietary tracking, remember to approach it with curiosity rather than judgment. Every meal is an opportunity to learn more about your body and how best to support your brain's function. Combining the insights from tracking with the nutritional strategies discussed in previous chapters, you can develop a personalized dietary approach to support your ADHD management and overall health.

In the next section of this workbook, we will explore behavioral strategies that can complement your dietary approach to managing ADHD. Remember, a holistic approach that addresses multiple aspects of lifestyle often yields the best results in controlling ADHD symptoms.

Chapter 29

Worksheets for ADHD Success Strategies

Practical tools are essential for implementing behavioral strategies that help manage ADHD. This chapter provides worksheets tailored to the strategies discussed in Sophia, James, Laura, and Nathan's stories. The worksheets are designed to guide readers in applying these methods to their own lives, encouraging self-reflection, planning, and action.

Worksheet 1: Sophia's Focus and Academic Success Worksheet

Goal: Create structure, manage tasks effectively, and reflect on academic progress.

Step 1: Daily Prioritization

- List your top 5 tasks for the day:

    1. _____
    2. _____
    3. _____
    4. _____
    5. _____

Step 2: Time-Blocking

- Allocate time slots for each task. Be realistic about how long each will take:
    - Task:_____|Time:_____
    - Task:_____|Time:_____

Step 3: Pomodoro Tracker
- Break tasks into 25-minute focus intervals. Use the table below to track your Pomodoros:

Task	Focus Interval (25 min)	Break (5 min)	Completed?
_____	_____	_____	_____
_____	_____	_____	_____

Step 4: Progress Reflection
- Reflect on your progress at the end of the day:
    - What went well today? _____
    - What could I improve tomorrow? _____

Worksheet 2: James' Prioritization and Balance Worksheet

Goal: Prioritize tasks effectively, set boundaries, and practice mindfulness to manage emotional stress.

Step 1: Task Categorization (Eisenhower Matrix)
- Sort tasks into the following quadrants:

Urgent & Important	Important but Not Urgent
_____	_____
_____	_____

Urgent but Not Important	Neither Urgent nor Important
_____	_____
_____	_____

Step 2: Boundary Setting

- List boundaries to maintain work-life balance:
  - I will not check emails after: _____
  - I will take breaks every: _____

Step 3: Daily Mindfulness Practice

- Set aside 5 minutes for mindfulness exercises. Use the prompts below:
  - What is one positive thing about today? _____
  - What can I let go of that is outside my control? _____

Worksheet 3: Laura's Holistic Management Worksheet

Goal: Balance professional responsibilities, personal life, and parenting with structure and communication strategies.

Step 1: Habit Stacking Planner

- Identify existing habits and stack new ones onto them:
  - Current Habit: _____
    New Habit: _____
  - Current Habit: _____
    New Habit: _____

Step 2: Visual Reminders and Chore Trackers

- Design a simple chore tracker or visual reminder system:
  - Task: _____ | Visual Cue: _____
  - Task: _____ | Visual Cue: _____

Step 3: Family Routine Checklist
- Create a routine for your household:
  - Morning:
    - Task 1: _____
    - Task 2: _____
  - Evening:
    - Task 1: _____
    - Task 2: _____

Step 4: Open Communication
- Weekly check-in questions:
  1. What went well this week? _____
  2. What can we improve next week? _____

Worksheet 4: Nathan's Wellness and Focus Worksheet

Goal: Balance hyperfocus with self-care and maintain a consistent routine.

Step 1: Time-Blocking for Breaks
- Schedule breaks into your workday to ensure balance:

Time	Activity
_____	_____
_____	_____
_____	_____

Step 2: Managing Hyperfocus
- Set time limits for tasks that might lead to hyperfocus:
  - Task:_____|Time Limit:_____
  - Task:_____|Time Limit:_____

Step 3: Meal Prep and Nutrition Tracker
- Plan your meals for the week and track your hydration:

Day	Breakfast	Lunch	Dinner	Snacks	Water Intake
Monday	_____	_____	_____	_____	_____
Tuesday	_____	_____	_____	_____	_____

Step 4: Self-Care Reflection
- Reflect on how well you managed self-care this week:
  - Did I take breaks? Yes / No
  - Did I stay hydrated? Yes / No
  - Did I prepare healthy meals? Yes / No

These worksheets are tools to help you take actionable steps toward managing ADHD effectively. Each worksheet reflects the strategies that worked for Sophia, James, Laura, and Nathan, offering a practical way to apply their lessons to your own life. Using these worksheets regularly can build habits that support focus, balance, and well-being.

Appendix
Additional Resources and Tools for ADHD Management

This appendix provides supplementary resources, tools, and information to help you deepen your understanding of ADHD and implement strategies for better organization, focus, and productivity. Use these resources to guide your journey toward effective ADHD management.

Section A: Recommended Books and Literature

1. For Understanding ADHD

    - Barkley, R. A. (2021). *Taking charge of ADHD: The complete, authoritative guide for parents.* Guilford Press.

    - Hallowell, E. M., & Ratey, J. J. (2011). *Driven to distraction: Recognizing and coping with attention deficit disorder from childhood through adulthood* (Revised ed.). Anchor Books.

2. For Emotional Regulation and Mindfulness

    - Zylowska, L. (2012). *The mindfulness prescription for adult ADHD: An 8-step program for strengthening attention, managing emotions, and achieving your goals.* Shambhala Publications.

    - Brown, T. E. (2014). *Smart but stuck: Emotions in teens and adults with ADHD.* Jossey-Bass.

3. For Women with ADHD

    - Quinn, P. O., & Nadeau, K. G. (2002). *Understanding women with ADHD.* Advantage Books.

- Solden, S. (1995). *Women with attention deficit disorder: Embrace your differences and transform your life.* Underwood Books.

4. For Lifestyle and Productivity
   - Ratey, J. J. (2008). *Spark: The revolutionary new science of exercise and the brain.* Little, Brown and Company.
   - Clear, J. (2018). *Atomic habits: An easy & proven way to build good habits & break bad ones.* Avery.

Section B: Recommended Apps and Tools

1. Task Management and Organization
   - Todoist: A versatile task management app that helps organize daily tasks and long-term projects.
   - Trello: A visual project management tool great for tracking progress on multiple tasks.

2. Focus and Productivity
   - Forest: A focus timer app using the Pomodoro technique to encourage sustained attention.
   - RescueTime: Tracks time spent on tasks and helps reduce distractions.

3. Mindfulness and Relaxation
   - Headspace: Guided meditations for improving focus and reducing stress.
   - Calm: Offers mindfulness exercises and relaxation tools for sleep and stress management.

4. Time Management
   - Google Calendar: A simple yet effective tool for scheduling and reminders.
   - Clockify: A time-tracking app to monitor how you spend your day.

Section C: Support Groups and Communities

1. Online Communities
   - ADHD Subreddit (r/ADHD): A supportive forum for sharing tips, experiences, and resources.
   - CHADD Forums: Online forums provided by Children and Adults with Attention-Deficit/Hyperactivity Disorder (CHADD).

2. Support Organizations
   - CHADD (Children and Adults with Attention-Deficit/Hyperactivity Disorder): www.chadd.org
   - ADDA (Attention Deficit Disorder Association): www.add.org

3. Local Support Groups
   - Many communities have local ADHD support groups. Search online or consult your healthcare provider for recommendations.

Section D: Worksheets and Templates

1. Daily Planner Template
   - Use a structured planner to organize your day with dedicated sections for tasks, appointments, and breaks.

2. Time-Blocking Template
   - Allocate specific time slots for each task using a simple time-blocking worksheet.

3. Habit Tracker
   - Track progress on new habits with a printable or app-based habit tracker.

4. Self-Reflection Journal
   - Use prompts to reflect on daily accomplishments and areas for improvement.

Section E: Frequently Asked Questions

Q1: How do I know if I need professional help for ADHD?
   - If ADHD symptoms significantly impair your ability to function at work, school, or in relationships, consider consulting a healthcare provider for an assessment.

Q2: Can ADHD be managed without medication?
   - While medication can be helpful, behavioral strategies, lifestyle changes, and coaching can also effectively manage ADHD symptoms. Many individuals use a combination of approaches.

Q3: How can I improve my focus at work?
   - Try techniques like the Pomodoro method, minimize distractions, and break tasks into smaller steps. Using apps like Forest or Trello can also help.

Q4: What should I do if I experience setbacks?
   - Remember, setbacks are part of the process. Reflect on what went wrong, adjust your strategies, and try again with patience and persistence.

Section F: Additional Research Articles

1. Tsitsipanis, C., et al. (2024). Remarkable recovery after severe gunshot brain injury: A comprehensive case study of functional rehabilitation. *American Journal of Case Reports, 25*, e941601. https://doi.org/10.12659/AJCR.941601
2. Volkow, N. D., et al. (2009). Imaging the dopamine system in ADHD: Diagnostic and therapeutic implications. *Journal of Clinical Psychiatry, 70* (Suppl 5), 3-8.
3. Frodl, T., & Skokauskas, N. (2012). Meta-analysis of structural MRI studies in children and adults with ADHD indicates a smaller right globus pallidus. *Brain Imaging and Behavior, 6*(4), 577-588. https://doi.org/10.1007/s11682-012-9173-2

This appendix is your go-to resource for enhancing your understanding of ADHD and accessing tools that support your journey. Use these resources to build momentum and stay on track with your goals. Remember, progress is a process, and every step forward counts!

References

1. American Psychiatric Association. (2013). *Diagnostic and statistical manual of mental disorders* (5th ed.). Arlington, VA: American Psychiatric Publishing.

2. Barkley, R. A. (2010). *ADHD in Adults: What the Science Says*. Guilford Press.

3. Barkley, R. A. (2010). *Taking Charge of Adult ADHD*. Guilford Press.

4. Barkley, R. A. (2017). *What Causes ADHD?*. Retrieved from https://www.russellbarkley.org/factsheets/WhatCausesADHD2017.pdf

5. Barkley, R. A. (2021). *Taking charge of ADHD: The complete, authoritative guide for parents* (4th ed.). Guilford Press.

6. Brown, T. E. (2005). *Attention Deficit Disorder: The Unfocused Mind in Children and Adults*. Yale University Press.

7. Brown, T. E. (2013). *A New Understanding of ADHD in Children and Adults: Executive Function Impairments*. Routledge.

8. Brown, T. E. (2014). *Smart but stuck: Emotions in teens and adults with ADHD*. Jossey-Bass.

9. Castellanos, F. X., Kelly, C., & Milham, M. P. (2008). The Restless Brain: Attention-Deficit Hyperactivity Disorder, Resting-State Functional Connectivity, and Intrasubject Variability. *Canadian Journal of Psychiatry, 54*(10), 665–672.

10. Castellanos, F. X., & Proal, E. (2012). Large-scale brain systems in ADHD: beyond the prefrontal–striatal model. *Trends in Cognitive Sciences*, 16(1), 17–26.

11. Cortese, S., Kelly, C., Chabernaud, C., Proal, E., Di Martino, A., Milham, M. P., & Castellanos, F. X. (2012). Toward systems neuroscience of ADHD: A meta-analysis of 55 fMRI studies. *The American Journal of Psychiatry, 169*(10), 1038–1055.

12. Cubillo, A., Halari, R., Ecker, C., Giampietro, V., Taylor, E., & Rubia, K. (2010). Reduced activation and inter-regional functional connectivity of fronto-striatal networks in adults with childhood Attention-Deficit Hyperactivity Disorder (ADHD) and persisting symptoms during tasks of motor inhibition and cognitive switching. *Journal of Psychiatric Research, 44*(10), 629–639.

13. Dodson, W. (2016). Secrets of the ADHD Brain. *ADDitude Magazine*. Retrieved from https://www.additudemag.com/secrets-of-the-adhd-brain/

14. Faraone, S. V., Asherson, P., Banaschewski, T., Biederman, J., Franke, B., Rohde, L. A., ... & Reif, A. (2015). Attention-deficit/hyperactivity disorder. *Nature Reviews Disease Primers, 1*, 15020. https://doi.org/10.1038/nrdp.2015.20

15. Faraone, S. V. (2005). Epidemiology of adult ADHD. *Journal of Clinical Psychiatry, 66*(Suppl 5), 3-7.

16. Fassbender, C., Schweitzer, J. B., Cortes, C. R., Tagamets, M. A., Windsor, T. A., & Mangun, G. R. (2009). Working memory in attention deficit/hyperactivity disorder is characterized by a lack of specialization of brain function. *PLoS One, 4*(11), e7220.

17. Frodl, T., & Skokauskas, N. (2012). Meta-analysis of structural MRI studies in children and adults with attention deficit hyperactivity disorder indicates smaller volumes in the right globus pallidus and putamen. *American Journal of Psychiatry, 169*(11), 1107-1116.

18. Goodman, D. W. (2007). The consequences of attention-deficit/hyperactivity disorder in adults. *Journal of Psychiatric Practice*, 13(5), 318–327.

19. Hallowell, E. M. (2020, July 20). *Feeding your ADHD brain... literally*. Dr. Hallowell. https://drhallowell.com/2020/07/20/feeding-your-adhd-brain-literally/

20. Hallowell, E. M., & Ratey, J. J. (2005). *Delivered from Distraction: Getting the Most out of Life with Attention Deficit Disorder*. Ballantine Books.

21. Hallowell, E. M., & Ratey, J. J. (2011). *Driven to distraction: Recognizing and coping with attention deficit disorder from childhood through adulthood* (Revised ed.). Anchor Books.

22. Hallowell, E. M., & Ratey, J. J. (2021). *ADHD 2.0: New Science and Essential Strategies for Thriving with Distraction—from Childhood through Adulthood*. Ballantine Books.

23. Hinshaw, S. P., & Scheffler, R. M. (2014). *The ADHD Explosion: Myths, Medication, Money, and Today's Push for Performance*. Oxford University Press.

24. Hinshaw, S. P. (2007). *The Mark of Shame: Stigma of Mental Illness and an Agenda for Change*. Oxford University Press.

25. Hoogman, M., Bralten, J., Hibar, D. P., Mennes, M., Zwiers, M. P., Schweren, L. S. J., ... & Franke, B. (2017). Subcortical brain volume differences in participants with attention deficit hyperactivity disorder in children and adults: a cross-sectional mega-analysis. *The Lancet Psychiatry, 4*(4), 310-319.

26. Hoza, B., Smith, A. L., Shoulberg, E. K., Linnea, K., Dorsch, T. E., Blazo, J. A., ... & McCabe, G. P. (2015). A randomized trial examining the effects of aerobic physical activity on attention-deficit/hyperactivity disorder symptoms in young children. *Journal of Abnormal Child Psychology, 43*(4), 655–667.

27. Klingberg, T., Fernell, E., Olesen, P. J., Johnson, M., Gustafsson, P., Dahlström, K., Gillberg, C. G., Forssberg, H., & Westerberg,

H. (2005). Computerized training of working memory in children with ADHD—A randomized, controlled trial. *Journal of the American Academy of Child & Adolescent Psychiatry, 44*(2), 177–186.

28. Konrad, A., Dielentheis, T. F., El Masri, D., Bayerl, M., Fehr, C., Gesierich, T., & Stoeter, P. (2010). White matter alterations in adult ADHD: A diffusion tensor imaging study. *Biological Psychiatry, 68*(12), 1234-1242.

29. Littman, E. B., & Quinn, P. O. (2015). *Understanding Girls with ADHD: How They Feel and Why They Do What They Do* (2nd ed.). Advantage Books.

30. Nadeau, K. G. (2015). *The ADHD Guide to Career Success: Harness Your Strengths, Manage Your Challenges*. Routledge.

31. Naidoo, U. (2020). *This Is Your Brain on Food: An Indispensable Guide to the Surprising Foods that Fight Depression, Anxiety, PTSD, OCD, ADHD, and More*. Little, Brown Spark.

32. Nigg, J. (2022, October 5). *ADHD and food dyes, nutrition, and supplements* [Webinar]. ADDitude Magazine. https://www.youtube.com/watch?v=XflDa1cKbns

33. Orlov, M. (2010). *The ADHD Effect on Marriage: Understand and Rebuild Your Relationship in Six Steps*. Specialty Press.

34. Owens, J. A., Saylor, K. E., Okano, L., & Hensley, M. (2013). The ADHD and sleep conundrum: A review. *Journal of Developmental & Behavioral Pediatrics, 34*(6), 382–392.

35. Posner, J., Marsh, R., Maia, T. V., Peterson, B. S., Gruber, A., & Simpson, H. B. (2011). Abnormal amygdalar activation and connectivity in adolescents with attention-deficit/hyperactivity disorder. *Journal of the American Academy of Child & Adolescent Psychiatry, 50*(8), 828–837.e3.

36. Quinn, P. O. (2001). *ADD and the College Student: A Guide for High School and College Students with Attention Deficit Disorder* (Rev. ed.). Magination Press.

37. Quinn, P. O., & Nadeau, K. G. (2002). *Understanding women with ADHD*. Advantage Books.

38. Ratey, J. J. (2008). *Spark: The revolutionary new science of exercise and the brain*. Little, Brown and Company.

39. Sarkis, S. M. (2015). *Natural Relief for Adult ADHD: Complementary Strategies for Increasing Focus, Attention, and Motivation With or Without Medication*. New Harbinger Publications.

40. Shaw, P., Eckstrand, K., Sharp, W., Blumenthal, J., Lerch, J. P., Greenstein, D., Clasen, L., Evans, A., Giedd, J., & Rapoport, J. L. (2007). Attention-deficit/hyperactivity disorder is characterized by a delay in cortical maturation. *Proceedings of the National Academy of Sciences of the United States of America, 104*(49), 19649–19654.

41. Solden, S. (1995). *Women with attention deficit disorder: Embrace your differences and transform your life*. Underwood Books.

42. Sonuga-Barke, E. J. S., & Castellanos, F. X. (2007). Spontaneous attentional fluctuations in impaired states and pathological conditions: A neurobiological hypothesis. *Neuroscience & Biobehavioral Reviews, 31*(7), 977–986.

43. Spencer, T. J., Brown, A., Seidman, L. J., Valera, E. M., Makris, N., Lomedico, A., & Faraone, S. V. (2013). Effect of psychostimulants on brain structure and function in ADHD: a qualitative literature review of magnetic resonance imaging-based neuroimaging studies. *The Journal of Clinical Psychiatry, 74*(9), 902–917.

44. Tsitsipanis, C., Papadimitriou, I., Tsoukaras, I., Moustakis, N., Lazarioti, S., Theofanopoulos, A. K., Kritikou, G., Ntotsikas, K., Simos, P., Kokkinakis, E., Karabetsos, D., & Vakis, A. (2024).

Remarkable recovery after severe gunshot brain injury: A comprehensive case study of functional rehabilitation. *American Journal of Case Reports, 25*, e941601. https://doi.org/10.12659/AJCR.941601

45. The Portland Clinic. (2015, November 10). *Like a growing number of people with attention-deficit/hyperactivity disorder (ADHD), Dr. Vanessa Welch-Pemberton was diagnosed in adulthood* [Facebook post]. Facebook. https://www.facebook.com/ThePortlandClinic/photos/like-a-growing-number-of-people-with-attention-deficithyperactivity-disorder-adh/972973714863629/

46. Tuckman, A. (2012). *Understand your brain, get more done: The ADHD executive functions workbook*. Specialty Press.

47. Tuckman, A. (Host). (n.d.). *What you don't remember... about your memory with Dr. Ari Tuckman* [Audio podcast]. ADHD reWired. Retrieved from https://www.youtube.com/watch?v=EmE0QAye_so

48. Volkow, N. D., Wang, G. J., Kollins, S. H., Wigal, T. L., Newcorn, J. H., Telang, F., Fowler, J. S., Zhu, W., Logan, J., Ma, Y., Pradhan, K., Wong, C., & Swanson, J. M. (2009). Evaluating dopamine reward pathway in ADHD: Clinical implications. *JAMA, 302*(10), 1084–1091.

49. Welch-Pemberton, V. (2015, November 10). *ADHD: My story*. The Portland Clinic. Retrieved from https://www.theportlandclinic.com/adhd-my-story/

50. Willcutt, E. G., Doyle, A. E., Nigg, J. T., Faraone, S. V., & Pennington, B. F. (2005). Validity of the executive function theory of attention-deficit/hyperactivity disorder: A meta-analytic review. *Biological Psychiatry, 57*(11), 1336–1346.

51. Wilens, T. E. (2004). Attention-deficit/hyperactivity disorder and the substance use disorders: the nature of the relationship, subtypes

at risk, and treatment issues. *The Psychiatric Clinics of North America, 27*(2), 283–301.

52. Wilens, T. E., Martelon, M., Joshi, G., Bateman, C., Fried, R., Petty, C., & Biederman, J. (2011). Does ADHD predict substance-use disorders? A 10-year follow-up study of young adults with ADHD. *Journal of the American Academy of Child & Adolescent Psychiatry, 50*(6), 543–553.

53. Wilens, T. E., & Spencer, T. J. (2010). Understanding attention-deficit/hyperactivity disorder from childhood to adulthood. *Postgraduate Medicine, 122*(5), 97-109. https://doi.org/10.3810/pgm.2010.09.2206

54. Young, J. L. (2007). *ADHD Grown Up: A Guide to Adolescent and Adult ADHD.* W. W. Norton & Company.

55. Zylowska, L., Ackerman, D. L., Yang, M. H., Futrell, J. L., Horton, N. L., Hale, T. S., Pataki, C., & Smalley, S. L. (2008). Mindfulness meditation training in adults and adolescents with ADHD: A feasibility study. *Journal of Attention Disorders, 11*(6), 737–746.

56. Zylowska, L. (2012). *The mindfulness prescription for adult ADHD: An 8-step program for strengthening attention, managing emotions, and achieving your goals.* Shambhala Publications.

www.ingramcontent.com/pod-product-compliance
Lightning Source LLC
LaVergne TN
LVHW041659070526
838199LV00045B/1124